HISPANIC BIOGRAPHIES

RUBÉN BLADES

Salsa Singer and Social Activist

Bárbara C. Cruz

Enslow Publishers, Inc.

44 Fadem Road   PO Box 38
Box 699   Aldershot
Springfield, NJ 07081   Hants GU12 6BP
USA   UK

Dedication
Para mi compañero en la salsa,
Kevin

Library of Congress Cataloging-in-Publication Data

Cruz, Bárbara C.
    Rubén Blades : Salsa singer and social activist / Bárbara C. Cruz.
        p. cm. — (Hispanic biographies)
    Includes filmography, discography, bibliographical references and
index.
    Summary: Traces the life of the international salsa singing star from
his early life in Panama through his career as a musician and actor and
his unsuccessful run for the presidency of his home country.
    ISBN 0-89490-893-6
    1. Blades, Rubén—Juvenile literature. 2. Singers—Panama—
Biography—Juvenile literature. 3. Salsa—History and criticism—
Juvenile literature. [1. Blades, Rubén. 2. Singers. 3. Panamanians—
United States—Biography.] I. Title. II. Series.
ML3930.B58C78   1997
782.42164'092—dc21
[B]   97-13031
                                                               CIP
                                                             AC MN
Printed in the United States of America

10 9 8 7 6 5 4 3 2

CONTENTS

ACKNOWLEDGMENTS

I would like to acknowledge the contributions of several individuals, without whose help this book would not have been possible:

Rubén Blades, who gave graciously of his time to be interviewed for this book;

Jack Vine, a keen editor, whose perspective in the writing of this series has been invaluable;

Robert G. Driver, for his skillful library sleuthing;

Elsa Acosta, for the best article clipping service anywhere, as well as her continued inspiration;

Kevin A. Yelvington, for his unwavering support and encouragement;

and finally, I would like to thank the anonymous reviewers whose very thoughtful and thorough evaluations improved the manuscript tremendously.

CHAPTER ONE

"I WANT TO SING!"

 Growing up in Panama, Rubén Blades was used to listening to all types of music. He especially liked the rock-and-roll songs from the United States that were regularly played on the radio. Most of the songs had catchy tunes, were fun to dance to, and were sung by young people. Since Rubén came of age in the late 1950s and early 1960s, he and his friends enjoyed listening to the songs of Elvis Presley, Bill Haley and the Comets, the Platters, Frankie Lymon and the Teenagers, and the Beatles.

Then something happened that changed Rubén's feelings toward the United States. In Panama, there is a ten-mile by fifty-mile strip of land known as the Canal Zone. It extends from the Atlantic port of Colón all the way to Panama City on the Pacific Ocean. The Panama Canal runs through it. The canal is a system of locks and gates that cuts through fifty miles of land, thereby connecting the Atlantic and Pacific Oceans. When it opened in 1914, it saved ships thousands of miles because they did not have to sail around the continent of South America. It takes ships about twelve hours to cross the canal.

The Canal Zone had long been a source of tension between the United States and Panama. According to a treaty signed in 1901, the United States was permitted to build and operate a canal across the isthmus (a narrow piece of land that connects two larger masses of land). Earlier, the United States had been instrumental in assisting Panama in breaking away from its colonial government, Colombia, in order to gain access to the canal.

Because of the Panama Canal, there were many Americans, both soldiers and civilians, who lived nearby in an area called the "Canal Zone." In a 1903 treaty, the United States was given complete power over the ten-mile strip "in perpetuity" (forever). While residents in the United States colony enjoyed prosperity and luxury, Panamanian citizens in the surrounding areas lived in poverty. Within the colony there was no unemployment, and United States workers were paid on a

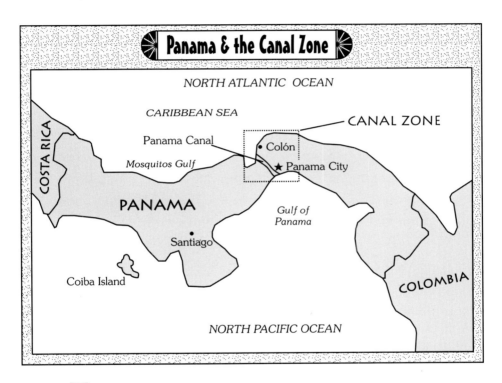

This map shows the location of the Canal Zone, occupied by the United States, within the country of Panama.

higher pay scale than non-United States workers. Many Panamanians also felt that it was unfair that the United States was getting richer from the traffic that went through the canal.

Panamanian citizens also started seeing newspaper photographs of snarling police dogs in Little Rock, Arkansas, in the first attempts to grant African Americans equal rights. Rubén remembers, "The period coincided with the Civil Rights movement [in the United States] and I saw pictures of dogs biting blacks because they were walking in a town. We never knew these things."[1] As a result, Rubén recalls that "people began to perceive the ugly side of this culture we all loved and wanted to be part of. At the same time, we started looking at ourselves more."[2]

One morning in January 1964, a few North American students attending Balboa High School in the Canal Zone refused to fly the Panamanian flag alongside the American, even though it was in violation of a United States-Panama agreement. In 1961 President John F. Kennedy had made an agreement with then Panamanian President Roberto Chiari that the Panamanian flag would be flown in the Canal Zone wherever the American flag flew. Yet on that January morning the American students chose not to honor that agreement.

The next day, in protest, two hundred Panamanian students from the National Institute marched into the

Canal Zone and tried to raise the Panamanian flag next to the American flag. The American Canal Zone students again refused, and when a fight broke out, the United States military was called to restore order. When police started attacking the Panamanian students with tear gas, a riot followed. Angry Panamanians stormed the Canal Zone, attacking the Panama City railway station and tearing down the border fence. The riot spread across the country, and other buildings such as the United States Embassy and the United States Information Agency were raided. The crowd attacked with sticks, stones, and homemade firebombs.

Fifteen-year-old Rubén was sickened by the news. He and his family gathered around the radio in the kitchen to hear the reports of the violence that was raging through the city. The United States troops were fighting back with clubs, dogs, and bullets. After four days of rioting, twenty-two Panamanians and three United States soldiers were left dead. Another five hundred Panamanian citizens were wounded and hundreds more were jailed. The International Commission of Jurists was called to investigate. The conclusion reached by the commission was that both sides were to blame, but that the American military and police used an excessive degree of force.[3]

Rubén could not believe that the "good guys" whom he had come to know through the movies and

In January 1964, riots broke out in the Panama Canal Zone when American students refused to fly the flag of Panama beside the American flag.

music had shot at his own people. He explained that "something snapped" in him and that there was a "tremendous loss of innocence."[4] Rubén said, "We couldn't justify this. How would I feel as a Panamanian trying to act as if nothing happened, when something had?"[5] Although Rubén acknowledges that he became less enchanted with the United States after the canal riots, he insists, "I also came to realize that a government and its people are different, and I never let any bitterness cloud my relationships with North Americans."[6]

It was then that Rubén became very interested in Latin American music and decided to write and sing in Spanish. "I stopped and looked at myself and realized that I was a Panamanian, and that my eyes weren't going to turn blue. I saw I had to deal with the reality of who I am."[7] Rubén explains:

> Personally, I like Sinatra very much, still do, still remember some of his standards. But after we had all the dead and wounded, the people of my country would have died if I had continued to worship the United States without asking questions of this culture. It would have been totally out of line for me to sing English songs and pretend like nothing had happened.[8]

Almost overnight, he turned his attention from American pop and rock and roll, and concentrated on the music of Latin America.

This is an aerial view of Panama City, where Rubén Blades was born.

During this time Rubén began listening to the Argentine singer Piero. Piero's songs had messages of social importance. Piero's music was about the problems and social issues that he saw in the neighborhoods of Argentina and that were relevant to people's lives. Rubén felt that "Piero wasn't the usual phony balladeer. His songs talked about social themes and issues, and gave glimpses of the neighborhood and the city. I realized that I could do the same thing with my reality."[9]

Piero had gained popularity with "Mi Viejo" ("My Old Man"), a timeless ballad that describes a man who can be found in any neighborhood, in any country. Indeed, the song has been recorded in Italy, Chile, and Brazil.[10] Later he recorded "Pedro Nadie" ("Pedro Nobody") based upon the loneliness and deep character of a real-life peasant who identified himself as just a nobody.

The Argentine singer was different from many of his contemporaries. He considered himself more of a storyteller than a singer. He was described by his partner in songwriting, José Tcherkaski, as an "anti-idol" because of the simple way he dressed and the passionate way he sang. "I am a testimonial singer," Piero once said. "My songs can be compared to newspaper chronicles that try to inform about things that are happening. If some of the songs reach the level of protest it is because something bad is happening in society, but it is not my intent to protest. Only to tell."[11]

Rubén was impressed by the strength of Piero's music and ideas. When Piero visited Panama, Rubén and a friend visited the Argentine singer at his hotel. Rubén thought that if he played a song he had written called "Pablo Pueblo," the musician might want to record it. The song was about the hard life of a factory worker whose "nourishment is hope." Since one of the meanings of the word *pueblo* is the common people, the song described the existence of many people throughout the Americas. Piero listened attentively as Rubén sang and played his guitar.

When he was finished, Piero said to Rubén, "I can't record this." Rubén, deeply disappointed, asked, "Why not?" Piero responded, "Because it's a good song and I want you to record it. That way there will be two of us."[12] Rubén vowed to himself that he would carry on in Piero's footsteps and deliver his message and his music to people all over the world.

CHAPTER TWO

GROWING UP IN PANAMA

Rubén Blades was born on July 16, 1948, in Panama City, Panama, to Anoland and Rubén Blades, Sr. He was the second of five children. The family lived in a working-class neighborhood, called San Felipe, that had red brick streets. It was close to the ten-mile strip occupied by the United States that was known as the Canal Zone. On the Fourth of July, Rubén could see the bright fireworks in celebration of the United States Independence Day.

His father's father, Reuben Blades, was from St. Lucia, a British colony in the Caribbean. He was an

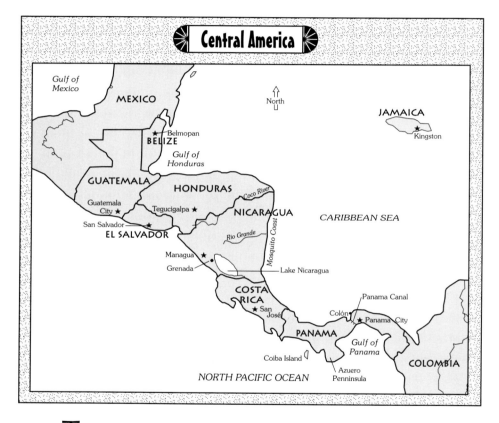

This map shows Panama, where Rubén Blades grew up, in relation to the other nations of Central America.

accountant and was drawn to Panama by the building of the railroad and the canal. In Panama, he met and married Emma Bosques Laurenza. Because Reuben was from an English-speaking island, the original pronunciation of his last name is in English, as in "razor blades," although most Latinos pronounce it "BLAH-dess." His grandson Rubén would come to accept both pronunciations. Emma's husband disappeared after fathering several children with her, including Rubén senior, Rubén's father. Rubén thinks that his grandfather left "after certain problems involving women."[1] Even though she was left to raise the family by herself, Rubén's grandmother, Emma, was a strong woman and was able to keep the family together.

Rubén's mother's father was an American named Joseph Louis Bellido de Luna. He was born in New Orleans and went to Cuba to fight in the Spanish-American War. Joseph liked the island so much that after the war he decided to stay and live there. Soon he met his future wife, Carmen Caramés, with whom he had twenty-two children. One of their daughters was named Anoland.

Rubén's mother, Anoland, was a piano player, nightclub singer, and radio actress in Cuba where she was born. She moved to Panama in the 1940s to perform in the nightclubs. One night she caught the eye of Rubén Blades, Sr., who was playing the bongo drums in the band she was singing with. Later, Rubén Blades,

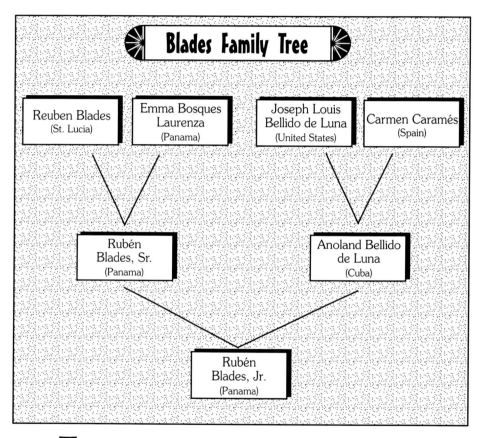

This is the Blades family tree, which shows the names and countries of origin of Rubén Blades's relatives.

Sr., was recruited to play on the National Secret Police's basketball team because he was such a good basketball player. Eventually he was enlisted as an officer by the National Secret Police in Panama and served as a detective for many years. After Rubén, Sr., and Anoland married, she put her musical training to use by giving piano lessons.

Growing up in Panama, Rubén's father's mother, Emma, had a powerful impact on him. Rubén has said of his *abuela* (grandmother) that she was a "wonderfully crazy woman who practiced levitation [making objects float in the air] and instilled in me the silly notion that justice is important, and that we can all serve and be part of the solution."[2] Rubén remembers his grandmother fondly, saying, "She was a very interesting, very special woman. She was obsessed with culture."[3]

It was Emma who taught Rubén how to read when he was just four years old by using comic books. He also remembers that his *abuela* would read to him from whatever she was reading and interested in at the time. After that, Rubén developed an intense interest in books. As he puts it, he read "anything and everything."[4] He especially liked fantasy and adventure novels such as *Tom Sawyer*, *20,000 Leagues Under the Sea*, *The Three Musketeers*, *The Iliad*, and *Treasure Island*. By age six, Rubén was studying Picasso and cubism. Cubism developed in Paris during the early

19

part of the twentieth century. In both painting and sculpture, cubism reduced objects and people to visually powerful geometric forms.

For her time, Emma was a very unusual woman. She was a writer, a painter, a poet, a vegetarian, a feminist, practiced yoga, and at a time when most girls did not go to school, had completed high school. She was one of the first women to graduate from high school in Panama. Emma sent her daughters to school, but not her sons. Rubén contends that: "She never had enough money, was barely making ends meet, but she felt it was a man's world, so she thought the women needed the education. The men she educated at home."[5]

Rubén's grandmother was also a Rosicrucian, a member of a secret religious organization based on mysticism. People who practice mysticism believe that there are realities beyond what humans are able to perceive just through intellect. Emma believed very strongly in spiritual powers. She also claimed she could make objects float without touching them. Emma also believed that she had lived before and in other lives was a slave in the Confederacy, a Roman soldier, and a French courtesan.[6] Once, Rubén and his family had to move from a home because his grandmother Emma believed it was teeming with ghosts.[7]

The summer days were very hot in Panama. Rubén and his *abuela* would sit in their cramped apartment

This is an aerial view of the Panama Canal, which caused so much controversy during Rubén Blades's childhood.

without even a ceiling fan to move the hot air. They would try fanning themselves with their little *abanicos* (hand fans) or a newspaper, but would still be very uncomfortable. To escape the heat, they would go to the Teatro Edison, and for fifteen cents each, would watch movies in the air-conditioned theater. His *abuela* would take him every day. This is how Rubén discovered American movies.

Later, Rubén described the theater:

> It had the coldest refrigeration system I have ever been in—in Panama, in New York, in Europe, anywhere on earth! That place was cold, man. You had to bring a jacket; there were penguins in the aisles! So we used to go every afternoon and watch movies all day. And they always used to show us, for reasons unknown to me, newsreels from Europe . . . in this theater filled with Panamanians trying to escape the heat![8]

While Rubén was growing up, there were many United States influences in Panama. Because the United States had been responsible for the construction and administration of the Panama Canal, there were many United States citizens who lived there. The Canal Zone included ten military bases, five thousand buildings, and ninety-three thousand acres of prime real estate on the banks of the Panama Canal. Within the Canal Zone, Americans enjoyed a prosperous life and had access to American goods, theaters, golf courses, and country clubs. It was sometimes called "a

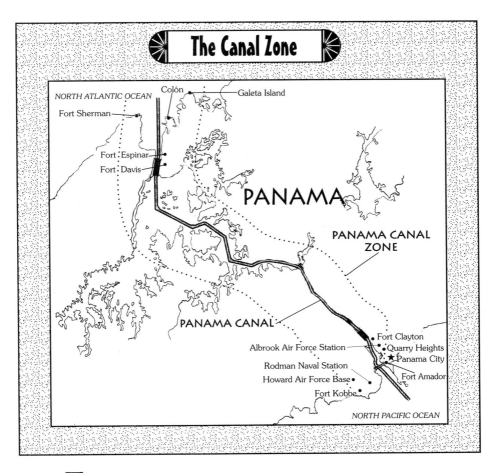

The Canal Zone

NORTH ATLANTIC OCEAN

Colón

Galeta Island

Fort Sherman

Fort Espinar

Fort Davis

PANAMA

PANAMA CANAL ZONE

PANAMA CANAL

Albrook Air Force Station

Rodman Naval Station

Howard Air Force Base

Fort Kobbe

Fort Clayton

Quarry Heights

Panama City

Fort Amador

NORTH PACIFIC OCEAN

This map shows the details of the Canal Zone, close to the childhood home of Rubén Blades.

country within a country." Even today, the United States dollar is used routinely to pay for goods even though the balboa is the official currency.

For entertainment, Rubén and his family mostly listened to the radio. Rubén remembers: "We were a radio family. In those days, you had a lot of time on your hands, so we would sit down wherever we could sit down in the house and listen to the radio."[9] Rubén grew up listening to the music of his parents. The songs of Latin American artists such as Beny Moré and Pérez Prado and flashy bands such as Orquesta Casino de la Playa filled the house. But the family also listened to the smooth, jazzy sounds of American musicians such as Nat King Cole, Dizzy Gillespie, Mel Tormé, Glenn Miller, and Duke Ellington.

In addition to Latin and American music, Rubén also listened to calypso music from the English-speaking Caribbean. Calypso is a type of Afro-Caribbean music that features humorous lyrics on social issues. Calypso songs often focus on current political events and poke fun at politicians. Rubén remembers: "As a kid I heard a lot of calypso: Lord Cobra, Lord Delicious, Mighty Sparrow. Well, there it was: calypso, in English, with an Afro-Cuban background. Still a commentary, because calypso is mainly social comment."[10]

During the 1950s and 1960s, when Rubén was growing up, rock-and-roll music was in its heyday.

Young Rubén Blades listened to the sounds of musicians like John Birks "Dizzy" Gillespie. This photograph of Gillespie was taken around 1955.

Rock-and-roll began to interest young people all over the world. Panama was no exception. In fact, Rubén proudly points out that because "Panama is a port, things hit there first."[11] Even though Rubén and his friends could not always understand the lyrics, they loved the instruments, vocals, and dances of the new music. They especially liked the fact that the artists were all young like themselves. Rubén recalled:

> The thing about rock 'n' roll was that it was played by young people. When we saw that, we went, "Wow!" because all the other music at the time was done by people whom we considered our elders. Rock 'n' roll was our music. The fact that it was produced in a different country, in a different language, didn't mean anything.[12]

Rubén and his friends listened to the songs of Elvis Presley, Bill Haley and the Comets, the Platters, and the Beatles on the radio. One of Rubén's favorite groups was Frankie Lymon and the Teenagers. They became popular with the song "Why Do Fools Fall in Love?" When Lymon and his group came to Panama City, Rubén was in the crowd of hundreds that greeted them at the airport. Rubén remembers that: "They were received like *kings*. Huge limos picked them up at the airport. The police were out front, with their sirens blaring. Everybody went to see them as if they were the president of the world!"[13]

Rubén was especially inspired by the fact that Lymon and his group consisted of three Puerto Rican

The Beatles were very popular in Panama, as they were around the world.

and two African-American teenagers from Harlem. This group of five African-American and Latino youths, led by fourteen-year-old Lymon, captured Rubén's imagination. He thought, "Wait a minute, we can do this, too!"[14] Rubén now says:

> Rock-and-roll in the mid-fifties was a turning point for many of us because it was the first music we'd heard made by people who were close to our own age. I remember seeing Frankie Lymon and the Teenagers in the movie *Rock, Rock, Rock.* They were kids who looked like guys that might have hung out on our corner. We were flabbergasted [amazed] that kids could do those things. Doo-wop records flooded the Panamanian market, and everybody started forming vocal groups and harmonizing in building entrances where they could find a good echo. For me it was a revelation to realize I didn't have to wait 'til I was 25 to be a musician.[15]

Rubén and his friends found a three-story building called the Audisio. They loved the second floor because of the wonderful way sound was carried in the high ceilings. Their parents were not very pleased, however, insisting, "Go to school! What are you doing singing in the hallways?"[16]

At the Lymon concert, Rubén sang along with the group from his seat, knowing all the words by heart. That's where he got an idea: He would write to Frankie Lymon and ask for an audition to be the sixth member of the group. He wrote the letter and asked his mother to mail it for him.

His mother, Anoland, did not want her son to become a musician. She wanted him to finish his education and then get a secure job. So, behind Rubén's back, she threw away the letter. When Rubén found out, he was furious. Realizing how important music was to her son, Anoland decided she would make it up to him. She bought Rubén a plastic guitar with a decal of Elvis Presley and a dog commemorating the hit song "Hound Dog."[17] Rubén started learning how to play the guitar on his own.

Spanish-speaking radio stations in Panama started playing songs by the Beatles in 1963. Rubén became fascinated with this group of young men from England. He decided that if the Beatles had been able to form a band, play in small clubs, and become famous, he and his friends could, too.

When Rubén was fifteen years old, he finally got a taste of what it was like to be in a rock-and-roll band. His older brother, Luis, was in a band called the Saints. One night the lead singer was not able to make it, and Luis asked Rubén to sing in his place. His mother Anoland was against it. She feared that Rubén would get used to the three or four dollars he would get paid and quit school. Rubén went anyway.[18]

The performance was a hit. The audience loved Rubén's singing. They also loved the music that came

As a boy, Rubén listened to Elvis Presley's music.

from the United States, listening to the songs on the radio. The Saints faithfully reproduced them in their act. After that, Rubén sang regularly with the Saints, singing popular American pop and rock-and-roll songs.

Later, Rubén recalled how he and his friends all looked up to the United States: "I admired the movies—Fred Astaire films, Bob Hope films . . . I admired the music—Elvis Presley, Bill Haley—the sense of liberty, the notion that you could do anything you wanted to do."[19] He also watched the TV show *Father Knows Best* and remembers thinking that everyone seemed "happy and they had ice cream in the icebox all the time."[20] Rubén remembers how he and all his friends grew up wanting to be North American: "We were watching an America we took literally to exist as such. A place where everything was always right. Everything was in Technicolor. Everybody had a car. Everything always had a happy ending."[21]

After the 1964 Panama Canal riots, Rubén decided he needed to rethink his beliefs: "I started re-evaluating, trying to educate myself not about the good things, which I already knew, but about the bad things."[22] In his spare time, he began to do more reading in history and politics.

Rubén started to become very interested in Latin music and decided to write and sing in Spanish. In particular, he looked to Latin musicians Ismael Rivera,

Mon Rivera, and Cortijo for inspiration. It was a turning point for Rubén. He shifted his attention away from American pop and rock-and-roll and began to concentrate on Latin music. After meeting the Argentine singer Piero, Rubén realized that he, too, could write songs about what he witnessed in his life and hopefully make a difference.

COMING TO
AMERICA

After graduating from high school, Rubén Blades enrolled in law school at the National University of Panama mostly to please his parents. Rubén, Sr., and Anoland wanted to make sure that their son would have a steady job in the future.

In 1968 he had made an album with an Afro-Cuban music group called Bush and the Magnificos. Pancho Cristal, a music producer in New York, heard the album. At the same time Cristal was looking for a replacement for the lead singer of Joe Cuba's band and offered Blades the job. Blades was very excited since Joe Cuba was one of the bands he had grown up listening to. Blades recalled, "The first Latin band I really liked was the Joe Cuba Sextet. They had a street sense in their songs along with a tremendous elegance."[1] Reluctantly, Blades turned the opportunity down because he had not yet finished his law degree. He hoped that it would not be his last chance at performing with a celebrated band.[2]

Blades remembers his years at the University of Panama as being difficult—having to study for his law degree and having to simultaneously work at a shipping agency. Even though during this time there were no tuition costs at the national university, his modest $50 monthly salary made it hard to make ends meet. He would have liked to have been involved in music during this time, but he realized that there was just no time to do so, given his studies and work obligations.[3]

This was a politically turbulent time in Panama. Arnulfo Arias was elected president of Panama in 1968. He was a medical doctor who had graduated from Harvard University in the United States. He had been president of Panama twice before, but ruled very harshly. The 1968 election was especially bitter. Each side accused the other of ballot tampering, and the National Guard ransacked Arias's headquarters. Arias himself called the 1968 campaign "one of the most shameful in the history of the country."[4] Although Arias won the election by a landslide, the country's powerful National Guard did not support his presidency.[5] Just ten days after he took office for the third time, Arias was overthrown in a military coup.

Very soon a military leader emerged; his name was Colonel Omar Torrijos Herrera. Torrijos proclaimed himself "maximum chief" and dissolved the National Assembly (congress). He eliminated political parties. Members of communist or revolutionary groups were arrested and jailed. Torrijos also enacted a constitution that put power in the hands of the military. As a result, the armed forces became the real authority in the country.

Nonetheless, Torrijos was a popular president. Even though he promoted a military government, he was also a charismatic leader who supported groups led by the people. He instituted a labor code that favored the workers. He encouraged the political participation of the lower classes for the first time. Torrijos put into operation a variety of social services and employment programs that benefitted poor people in urban shanty towns as well as those in the country.

Panamanians also supported his position on the Panama Canal. Early on, Torrijos made it clear that he wanted Panama to gain complete authority over the canal. In a speech before two hundred thousand people he asked, "What country or people in the world supports the humiliation of a foreign flag nailed in its heart?"[6] He became a national hero when he negotiated and signed the treaty that would give Panama full control over the Panama Canal by the end of the century. The marker on Torrijos's grave in Panama City reads: "I don't want to enter the history books. I want to enter the Canal Zone."

Yet the people's immediate reaction to the 1968 military coup was negative. Despite his social reforms, Torrijos abused his military power. As a response to the military's repressive actions, university students and faculty issued a declaration criticizing the overthrow. This document was signed by the university students, faculty members, and administrators. In protest, they marched. There was a confrontation between them and the Panamanian army. Student leaders were arrested, along with two hundred other people. As a result of the protest, the government occupied the campus and closed the university for one year.

When the university was shut down, Blades contacted his brother Luis, who was an airline employee. With Luis's help, Blades was able to buy a low-cost ticket and go to the United States. By 1969 he was in New York in the middle of the music scene.

During this time there was a great increase in the popularity of music from Latin America. By the late 1960s there was an immense growth in the number of Latinos who were already living and working in the United States. These new Americans, who had emigrated from Central and South America and the

This is one of the Hispanic neighborhoods in New York City, where people like Rubén Blades blended the culture of their native countries with the American culture.

Caribbean, brought with them their heritage and cultural practices, one of which was music.

Musicians such as Tito Puente, Machito, and Willie Colón were instrumental in developing the music known as *salsa*. Salsa music—a rich blend of African rhythms, Spanish guitar, and North American jazz, rock, and rhythm and blues—was created by Latinos in the United States. It has been said that salsa was born in the New York *barrio* (a mostly Spanish-speaking community or neighborhood).

Salsa means a spicy or flavorful sauce in Spanish. Charlie Palmieri, the New-York-born Puerto-Rican pianist, explains: "*Salsa* means literally a sauce, the kind your mother makes. It's hot and spicy and that's how we describe our music."[7] Salsa songs are dance tunes, usually upbeat and fun. The salsa band is smaller than traditional bands from Latin America, which often were more the size of orchestras.

The 1960s in particular were an important decade for the salsa movement. Latinos joined the ranks of African Americans, women, and others who called for equality and social change. In New York, a group of activists was formed called the Young Lords. The Young Lords were important not only in demanding fair treatment for Latinos, but also for promoting pride in being Latino.[8]

After seeing and hearing the great salsa musicians in New York City, Blades decided he had a contribution to make. He looked up music producer Pancho Cristal, who had contacted him earlier to join Joe Cuba's band, and was soon on his way to making an album.

Blades cut his first album in 1970 with Pete Rodríguez, a bugalú artist. *Bugalú*, also known as "Latin-soul," was a music and dance style popular in the 1960s. It blended African-American and Afro-Cuban rhythms; sometimes the lyrics were in English. Blades and Rodríguez's album was called *De Panamá a Nueva York: Pete Rodríguez Presenta a Rubén Blades* ("From Panama to New York: Pete Rodríguez Presents Rubén Blades"). With the exception of one song, Blades wrote all the lyrics on the album. Unfortunately, bugalú was fading in popularity, and the album did not sell well. Blades was disappointed.[9]

Soon Blades heard that the university had reopened in Panama and he decided to return and finish his law degree. In 1972 he received his degree from the University of Panama, the first person in his family to graduate from college. Blades explains: "I didn't study because of a simple interest in law, but because it keeps you out of the ghetto. It validates your intelligence. The diploma demands respect. It's an intellectual .38 [gun]."[10] Upon graduation, he set out to find a job as an attorney.

Blades worked for a while as an attorney for the Banco Nacional de Panamá, the national bank of Panama. During this time he also volunteered many

It was the sounds of great salsa musicians like Tito Puente (pictured above left) that inspired Rubén Blades to pursue a career as a salsa singer.

hours counseling prisoners. As much as Blades felt that he was doing important work, however, he was becoming dissatisfied. During his off-time, he started writing his own songs and performing with local bands.

Then something happened that greatly affected his family. General Manuel Antonio Noriega was the military strongman in the Torrijos government. During this time, Blades's father was a secret policeman for the government. In 1973 Noriega accused Rubén, Sr., of working for the Central Intelligence Agency (CIA) of the United States.[11] Blades's father denounced the charge as untrue and left Panama with his wife Anoland and their four children. They moved to Miami, Florida, where there was a thriving Latino community. However, because of his job, Blades himself decided to stay in Panama.

Yet, as he continued to play with salsa bands, it was not long before he dreamed of returning to New York and joining the salsa scene. New York attracted Latin musicians, composers, and performers from all over the world. In addition to the recording industry and nightclubs that were there, there were also Spanish-speaking *bodegas* (small grocery stores), *barrios* (Latino neighborhoods), and opportunities for employment.

After two years of working as an attorney, Blades quit his job. In 1974 he decided that New York was where he wanted to be and where he could make the most difference. Blades says:

> I felt that popular music would play an important role in Latin America. I felt it was an effective way of stating cases, of presenting the truth, the people's side, because they all had sounds, and those sounds were as important as anything I could do in a court of law.[12]

He also explained that he could not be a recording musician back home in Panama because the country did not have the recording studios, record distributors, or producers that were readily available in the United States.

Blades arrived in New York with just $100 in his pocket. Soon, however, he accepted a job with the Panamanian consulate in New York. His parents were pleased that he was working in a position that might lead to a career in the Panamanian foreign service.[13] Blades was doing so well, in fact, that he was offered an assignment in the Panamanian embassy in Washington, D.C. Still he realized that although it would be an important position, he would be moving farther away from a musical career. Blades decided that he would stay in New York. Yet how could he break into the salsa scene?

SALSA WITH A MESSAGE

Rubén Blades has always felt that music is one way he can have a positive influence on people: "I've always believed that music can do more than offer an escape—it can help bring people together to change their lives."[1] In 1974 he decided to begin concentrating on developing his own singing style based on the patterns set by Tito Rodríguez and Cheo Feliciano, two accomplished Puerto-Rican musicians.[2]

At first Blades worked in the mailroom of New York's leading salsa record company, Fania Records. Part of his job required him to push a large cart full of mail from 57th Street and Broadway to 52nd Street every day. His starting salary was $73 a week. Blades found a small apartment on the Upper West Side and furnished it simply, even using some discarded objects that he found on the street. After work he would visit all the salsa nightclubs. There he heard great salsa musicians such as Tito Puente, Ray Barretto, Johnny Pacheco, Willie Colón, and Charlie and Eddie Palmieri.

After working at Fania for a few months he got his big break. Ray Barretto, a conga player and band-leader born in Brooklyn, called Blades to say that he needed a backup singer. Blades was delighted and soon he began to sing traditional salsa with Ray Barretto's band. He made his debut in 1974 at Madison Square Garden. Because he was so nervous, Blades missed several of his cues while he was onstage, but the audience responded to him positively anyway.[3]

During his free time Blades also started writing songs about social issues and Hispanic pride and unity. This was very different from the light and upbeat dance tunes that made up salsa music at the time. Blades is widely credited as being the first salsa singer to write his own songs and the first to include politics in his music. He says of his decision to write socially relevant music:

> I think that for too long this business has been run by people who don't understand the music. They

It was conga player and bandleader Ray Barretto who gave Rubén Blades his first big break, singing traditional salsa with Barretto's band.

always felt the less you say, the better off you will be. In other words, don't get too deep because people don't understand that, they don't want to be bothered by it. It's also the case that a lot of musicians—and I'm sorry to say this—are not too creative. They fall into a pattern that works and they stay there. That is one of the reasons I got involved with salsa music.[4]

In 1976 Blades began to collaborate with the Bronx *salsero* (salsa musician) Willie Colón. Colón was born in New York and began playing the trumpet when he was twelve. Two years later he switched to the trombone and put a band together. When he was just fifteen he was signed by Fania Records. As a teenager in 1967, he recorded his first album, *El Malo*, which got him the nickname "El Niño Malo" (The Bad Boy). The record went on to sell more than thirty thousand copies. Colón went on to develop "gangster-salsa," which told the stories of the macho hoodlums in the barrio. One of Colón's later albums had a cover that was fashioned after an FBI "wanted" poster. Colón was declared to be "armed with trombone and considered dangerous."[5]

By the time Blades and Colón met, Colón had already caused a shake-up in the salsa industry. First, he had given up the traditional tuxedos and dark suits that most Latin bands wore, and replaced them with more casual clothing. Colón tells how his mother dyed some shirts pink and with a magic marker printed the

Salsa musician Willie Colón collaborated on musical projects with Blades for several years. Colón was famous for "shaking up" the salsa music industry.

band's name across the back.[6] He also improvised a lot and used several different rhythms in the same song. Colón recalled:

> . . . when I started a song with a Puerto Rican *aguinaldo* [Puerto Rican Christmas carol] that went into a Cuban *son montuno* [popular dance music of twentieth century Cuba] and then into a Dominican *merengue* [national music and dance of the Dominican Republic], with occasional English or Spanglish [combination of Spanish and English] choruses, nobody flinched . . . except for some of the old timers who nearly had apoplexy [a fit or seizure]. It was blasphemous! It was incorrect! It was . . . *Salsa!*[7]

In 1977 Blades and Colón collaborated to produce *Willie Colón Presents Rubén Blades*. The combination of Blades's songs and Colón's arrangements created a revolution in the salsa movement. They went on to create four gold albums. Their album *Siembra*, produced in 1978, is considered to be the best-selling salsa album in history, selling over 3 million copies. One of the songs from that album, "Pedro Navaja," based on "Mack the Knife," is still so popular that fans clamor for it by name at concerts.

The typical structure of salsa songs features call-and-response patterns that have their background in African music. Call-and-response is when the *coro* (chorus) repeats a key phrase in response to the lead singer. Many times the words conjured up traditional scenes from Latin America. Blades remembers:

> I used to hear the bands play an old song, which typically went: "On the golden hill, the rooster wakes you up." I thought, hey, wait a minute. Most of these people never set foot on a mountain. And it's not a rooster that wakes them up, but a G.E. alarm clock.[8]

Frank M. Figueroa, who has written an encyclopedia of Latin American music in New York, confirms that "very few attempts were made to depict the reality of life in New York in the music that was played."[9]

Blades had dreams of creating music that would carry strong social messages and would appeal to Anglo-Americans as well. He feels that his songs are "popular literature that is sung."[10] As one reviewer put it, the main message of Blades's songs is "to stimulate thought, to raise consciousness."[11] One journalist observed that Blades's songs "are not of partying, but of protest."[12]

Blades was instrumental in developing one of the varieties of salsa known as *salsa conciente*. This is salsa with a message. It highlights the social concerns faced by people in the barrios everywhere. There are even some salsa bands called *La Justicia*, *La Protesta*, and *La Conspiración* who, by their very names, suggest their interest in justice, political protest, and conspiracy against disempowered groups. Rubén Blades and

Willie Colón have written some of the best examples of this type of salsa.[13]

Blades says that 90 percent of the time his songs begin with the lyrics, or words.[14] He says that he has a drawer in which he keeps little bits of paper with words and ideas scribbled on them.

> Once in a while, I look at them, and if there's that burst of enthusiasm, I know it's time to do the song; it's like they hatch themselves. When I have enough good ones, I call the guys and say, "Okay, write the charts and let's go to the studio."[15]

Mainly, the songs protest political corruption and greed for power and money, and highlight social issues such as deforestation and AIDS. Blades says, "Salsa is light stuff. It's to help you forget. I make people think. They support it or condemn it, but they react."[16]

After hearing his songs, recording companies and dance club owners told Blades that his songs were "too long and too depressing." Yet Blades remembered that Piero, one of the singers who had inspired him, had also been told by record companies that he needed to sing more upbeat, popular music instead of songs with social messages. Blades held on to his vision that he could use salsa music "to confront, not to escape."[17]

The lead singer in a salsa band has a very important position. Lead singers often become the stars of the band. They are usually required to play the *maracas*, too. Maracas are a pair of gourds (the dried and hollowed

This a typical street scene in New York City, where Blades went to begin his career as a musician.

out shells of calabash fruit such as pumpkin or squash) filled with seeds. When they are shaken rhythmically, they lend an identifiable beat to the music. Maracas have been used throughout the Caribbean and Latin America since pre-Columbian times.[18]

Fania Records had been formed in 1964 by the Dominican-American musician Johnny Pacheco; he was later joined by the Italian-American attorney and businessman Jerry Masucci in 1967. They signed artists from all over Latin America and brought them to New York to record music albums. Fania Records was one of the first music producers that promoted the term *salsa*.[19]

Recognizing that the lead singers in their salsa bands were very important, Fania organized them into a group called the Fania All-Stars. Blades was one of the musicians chosen and he had the opportunity to perform with salsa greats such as Celia Cruz, Johnny Pacheco, and "the high priest of salsa music," Tito Puente. The group toured internationally, and Blades was able to visit many countries.

After five very successful years, Blades officially broke with Colón in 1982. When asked why they went separate ways, Blades responded that he had interests in other things such as pursuing his graduate education and career in films. He felt that it would be unfair to ask his partner to wait patiently while he explored these other interests.[20]

52

Rubén Blades (shown above) broke off his partnership with Willie Colón in 1982 to pursue his interests in furthering his education and performing on his own.

Soon Blades became disillusioned with Fania. The managers at the record company wanted the musicians to produce traditional salsa. Many of them, Blades included, found that their creativity was being stifled by Fania's tight control and conservatism. Blades also disagreed with Fania about how the profits were distributed. Using his legal training, Blades sued the record company for royalties that he felt he deserved. He was able to win back some of the money and also received the copyrights to all the songs that he had written. Blades then tried to start a union on behalf of salsa musicians, but he was unsuccessful.[21] Nevertheless, Blades's lawsuit against Fania was valuable in empowering other Latino musicians and dealing with past abuses. The record company never fully recovered after the lawsuit.

In establishing his independence, Blades created his own band in 1982, a sextet he named "Seis del Solar." The name of the group is translated by some as "the Street Lot Six," but is more accurately interpreted as "Six from the Tenement" or "Six from the 'Hood." *Solar* really means the local neighborhood. With his new band, Blades now really had the opportunity to create the music he always dreamed of.

SEIS DEL SOLAR

Seis del Solar has been called "the most unusual band in salsa."[1] In part, that is because of the instruments they use. In traditional salsa groups, there are one or two lead singers, two to five brass instruments (such as trumpets and trombones), piano, bass, conga drums, timbales, bongo drums, a cowbell, and other small percussion instruments. Seis del Solar, however, replaced the horns with synthesizers, allowing the band to be composed of just six members as opposed to the usual larger salsa band format. Blades also added vibraphones and a trap set (the usual drum setup for pop and rock bands). Blades's decision to incorporate this into the percussion section is significant because it makes a "musical and visual statement of his own special role of crossing over aesthetically and culturally."[2]

One music writer feels that by replacing the brass with vibes, the music has "an airier feel that helps focus more attention on the lyrics."[3] The group also enhanced the primary Afro-Cuban musical base by adding elements of jazz, rock, 1950s doo-wop, and other Latin American beats. This new musical style Blades calls "urban music" and expresses "the feeling of the Latin American city dweller—his anguish, his hopes, his happiness, and his pain."[4] Blades feels that salsa music is "the folklore of the city—not of one city, but of all cities in Latin America."[5]

The songs written by Blades and sung with Seis del Solar were instantly popular with the Latino populations in many places. One reviewer commented that: "Blades's poignant [powerful] stories from street level are hitting the young, aware Hispanic community right in the gut."[6] Blades himself has said that a great inspiration for the lyrics and the rhythm come from *la esquina*—"the corner where people hang out."[7] Many of his songs are stories about life in the barrio. In 1984 he was given the opportunity to share these stories with listeners throughout the world.

Blades was the first salsero signed by a mainstream label (Elektra/Asylum). He explained that his aim was not to make a crossover album, but to "make an urban American album that can be appreciated by any American city dweller and may bring people who haven't identified with salsa a bit closer to us."[8]

In 1984 his album *Buscando América* ("Searching for America") sold 300,000 copies in the first five months and was nominated for a Grammy Award. The album also made it on *Time* magazine's list of the ten best rock albums of the year. The success of *Buscando América* was surprising because, unlike most salsa music, which are dance and party tunes, the songs on Rubén's album are serious and complicated.[9] One music writer feels that Blades's poetic lyrics are unique because they tell simple stories, often with political messages.[10]

Buscando América is a record of life in the barrios throughout North, Central, and South America.[11] It features mythical personalities that are well known to Latinos throughout the Americas—Pablo Pueblo, a factory worker; Juan Pachanga, a playboy; Ligia Elena, a society girl who runs away. The album also pays tribute to Blades's varied musical background. The album has traces of doo-wop, rock and roll, jazz, and calypso.

Although the songs in *Buscando América* are sung in Spanish, the liner notes provide the English translation. Blades insisted that this be done so that everyone could understand the messages of the songs. He explained: "I had the lyrics translated into English for the cover because I'm obsessed with clarity. . . . I believe it's everybody's duty to make the effort to be understood."[12] Ever since then, Blades has made sure that each of his albums provides the lyrics in both English and Spanish.

Buscando América was controversial in several ways. One song, "El Padre Antonio y el Monaguillo Andrés," tells about a priest murdered at the altar and is based on the real-life assassination of Archbishop Oscar Arnulfo Romero. Archbishop Romero had been outspoken in his criticism of the Salvadoran government's abuse of its citizens' political rights. As he was conducting mass at the San Salvador Cathedral in El Salvador, he was shot and killed. When Blades heard about the murder, he decided to write a song about it, in part to come to terms with his feelings and in part to express his outrage. He worked on the song for nine months, carefully writing the lyrics.[13]

In another song, Blades criticizes the dictatorship of General Manuel Antonio Noriega. When President Omar Torrijos died in a mysterious plane crash in 1981, Noriega, who was head of the Panamanian Defense Forces, created a corrupt military dictatorship in Panama. He was eventually overthrown by a United States invasion in 1989. Twenty-three United States soldiers and hundreds of Panamanians were killed, although human rights organizations have estimated the number of Panamanians who died as a result of the invasion to be as high as 3,000 to 4,000. The invasion caused about $2 billion worth of damage.[14] Noriega was captured, brought to the United States, and tried on federal drug charges. Noriega is now serving a forty-year drug-trafficking sentence in the United States. Several of his aides are still awaiting trial on charges of abuses.

A poll taken shortly after the invasion showed that more than 90 percent of Panamanians approved of it. In fact, one government official remarked that when he saw the United States soldiers parachuting into Panama City, they reminded him "of angels falling from the sky."[15] However, not everyone in Panama agreed with "Operation Just Cause," as President George Bush called it. There was a public outcry in the United States as well. One 1992 documentary, *The Panama Deception*, presents evidence that civilian casualties and internment was concealed by the United States military. The film also maintains that the United States' secret agenda was to keep United States military bases in Panama after the year 2000. Blades criticized the United States invasion of Panama, calling it an outrageous violation of international law.[16]

Another of Blades's songs, "Decisiones," makes reference to a woman's missed menstrual period and the decision that must be made. In Panama, "Decisiones" produced a debate about its appropriateness. In the song, a young woman worries she might be pregnant and contemplates her "decision." Even though the song does not advocate a particular course of action, censors in Panama felt that the song was promoting abortion and banned the song. When Blades performed in Panama in 1985, he was prohibited from playing the song.

"Desapariciones" tells about the "disappeared" people in countries such as Chile, Argentina, and El Salvador who are kidnapped and killed by the army because they have differing beliefs than the government. Friends and family of the disappeared have attracted international attention by protesting in unusual ways, such as dancing solo (to show that they are missing their partner), going on hunger strikes, and by sewing *arpilleras* (traditional quilts). Blades's song describes the piercing pain that relatives experience when their thoughts "bring them back."

A related song on the album, "GDBD," is perhaps the most eerie track. The song describes the morning of a typical man as he is getting ready to go to work. The listener can easily sympathize with all the little problems he encounters—the little razor cuts as he shaves his face, having to retie his tie because it does not come out right the first time, remembering that bills are due. What is chilling is that at the end, the listener realizes that the man is a secret police agent on his way to make a political arrest of the kind described in "Desapariciones." The work of the Austrian novelist Franz Kafka served as an inspiration for "GDBD." Blades explains: "You identify with the guy in this song, and then you find out what he does for a living and you go, 'Oh, my God, how could I compare myself to him?' And that's the whole point of it: We're all capable of that."[17]

"El Tiburón" ("The Shark") criticizes the United States' role and actions in Central America. Blades, like many other Latin Americans, has been vocal about United States involvement in the region.

> My contra-intervention themes [the shark who never gets full] are not directed exclusively to the United States policy in Latin America, but include the Russians in Afghanistan and the British in Argentina. I didn't make it up—it's history! All I'm saying is, "Leave us alone!"[18]

The song caused controversy in Miami's politically conservative Little Havana community. A popular Spanish-language radio station in Miami brought Blades to Miami to perform at a concert but asked him not to sing "El Tiburón." Blades refused to be censored, however, and sang the song anyway while wearing a bulletproof jacket. The radio station claims that they received bomb threats and banned "El Tiburón" from their programming.[19] Other radio stations banned his music altogether. Blades was also upset that his parents, who had moved to Miami, became caught up in the controversy and received threatening letters and calls. As a result, Blades refused to play in Miami in the future. He has, however, played at surprise jam sessions at Café Nostalgia, a nightclub dedicated to playing Cuban music from the 1930s, 1940s, and 1950s.

Blades could not understand why the Miami Cuban community would be so upset at him, since he has said on many occasions that he is opposed to Cuba's communist government. Blades points out the inherent contradictions in complaining about the repressive regime in Cuba, yet banning his records. He insists that he "resents it with all his heart."[20] He has also declared that he himself is not communist, although he acknowledges that his position on certain issues—such as health, housing, and education—is aligned more with the political left.[21] Communism is a system in which property is owned in common. That means that all farms, factories, and other property are owned by the government to benefit all people. When one is a "leftist" in politics, it means that one supports egalitarian goals for all people by reforming the current system.

Blades's 1985 album *Escenas* was a more personal work that explored relationships. He said, "Everything I wrote for *Escenas* is something I've seen and felt."[22] Many of the songs describe how people often feel

This photograph is of Little Havana in Miami, Florida, where the controversy over Blades's song "El Tiburón" was so strong that Blades refused to play in Miami again.

lonely, bored, and scared of being abandoned. In "Silencios," a duet sung in Spanish with Linda Ronstadt, he describes a couple whose love is dying. He explained:

> One of the biggest problems in Latin America today is that we seldom take the time to explore our own selves. When it comes to everyday relationships, men and women just don't understand each other, and from that lack of understanding comes the confusion of who you are in society, your direction and responsibilities.[23]

Despite the sometimes negative or dismal outlook in some of the songs, *Escenas* includes a very upbeat piece called "Muévete." This song is a plea to Latinos everywhere to join forces and "Get Moving."

Many salsa singers, including Blades, use a variety of Latin American rhythms in their songs. They may alternate among Afro-Cuban, Puerto-Rican, Dominican, and Brazilian rhythms within just one song. In addition to the musical reasons for using such a combination, there is a political one as well. Blades and other salsa singers would like to see a unified Latin American and Hispanic people. As Charley Gerard and Marty Sheller note in their book *Salsa!*: "These are all our rhythms, regardless of their local origin. Just as we can combine these rhythms together and rise above their differences, we can rise above the regional differences and become One People."[24] Many of Blades's songs "identify with the victims of oppression—not of any particular country, for Rubén Blades looks at the Hispanic people as a whole, not according to separate nations."[25]

In 1987 Seis del Solar released *Agua de Luna*. These songs written by Blades are loosely based on Nobel Prize winner Gabriel García Márquez's collection of stories. Blades met the author in Mexico in 1985 and they have remained friends since. García Márquez told a friend: "Through Rubén's songs, I'm going to be the singer I never was."[26] Says Blades of García Márquez: "I love him not because of his skills but because he is an intellectual who likes salsa music—he has kept one foot in the popular culture."[27]

In creating *Agua de Luna*, Blades thought it would be interesting to bring together literature and rhythmic music, two forms of culture that he feels have been commonly believed to be opposite. "And," Blades adds, "I always thought that was a bunch of crap because even intellectuals need to dance."[28] He joked with García Márquez that he was going to put a little sticker on the album that said "You heard the song. Now read the book." The author got a good chuckle when he heard Blades's proposal.[29]

Some people were disappointed that *Agua de Luna* was not a direct adaptation of the author's stories. Blades explains that "The songs don't retell the stories but express the emotions I felt reading them."[30] García Márquez defended Blades's work and added, "If I were a Panamanian, I would vote for him as president of the Republic."[31] Gabriel García Márquez calls him "the most popular unknown I've ever known."[32]

Nothing But the Truth was Blades's first record in English. It was released in 1988. Other popular singers such as Sting, Elvis Costello, Eric Clapton, and Lou Reed appeared on the album and helped him write some of the songs, too. Many of the tunes address important social issues such as AIDS ("The Letter") and human rights violations ("Salvador"). He also sarcastically comments on Oliver North's involvement in the Iran-Contra scandal in the song "Ollie's Doo-Wop."

The album was also unusual in that it included eleven different styles of songs. Blades got the idea from his childhood experience of listening to radio in Panama: "I wanted to present a whole fabric of different colors and sounds and put them together on a record the way I remembered radio to be when radio played all different kinds of music."[33]

By 1989 Blades's group was known as "Son del Solar" ("Sound of the Tenement") and had added a seventh member. *Son* is also a type of music that is very popular throughout Latin America, and especially Cuba. The new band has been described as "tight as a conga skin and hot as you can get."[34] The new group's first album was *Antecedente*. It was recorded in

Spanish and paid tribute to the group's Latin American heritage.

In 1993 Blades released *Amor y Control*. One song, "Naturaleza Muerta" ("Still Life"), explores what it would be like if the last tree in the Brazilian forest were to be chopped down. Another song, "Conmemorando" ("Commemorating"), argues that Columbus's lust for gold and passion for conquest should not be celebrated, but merely commemorated or simply observed.

Amor y Control also has several personal tracks. In "West Indian Man," Blades pays tribute to his paternal grandfather. Two songs, "Amor y Control" ("Love and Control") and "Canto a la Madre" ("Song to Mother"), express his love and sadness at the death of his mother. The inscription on the back of the album simply says "I dedicate this album to my mother Anoland. May she rest in peace." Blades has said:

> I think artists become artists because they're seeking some kind of love or affection. There's some kind of insecurity that can only be alleviated or resolved through approval from an external source. I think I became a singer because there was something lacking in my emotional life.[35]

Blades's latest album is *La Rosa de los Vientos*, which incorporates many different musical styles and instruments. He was able to record the album in his native Panama. The songs are heavily influenced by

Afro-Cuban music and rock and roll. Blades has performed in dozens of concerts in countries all over the world, such as France, Mexico, Switzerland, Germany, Ecuador, and Colombia. His 1986 debut at Carnegie Hall in New York City drew a sold-out crowd. In Latin America he attracts up to forty thousand fans at a single concert.[36] Many of the concerts are for a social cause and he performs for free. He has done concerts to benefit causes such as the homeless, AIDS awareness, the battle against drugs, and apartheid, among others. Blades proudly claims, "Nobody does more benefits than me."[37]

Music critics say that "More than any other single person, he [Blades] has managed to both revitalize Latin music and bring it to the attention of the non-Spanish-speaking public."[38] Since the 1950s other salsa artists have tried to reach Anglo audiences. Joe Cuba, Ray Barretto, Eddie Palmieri, and others attempted it, but with little success. Blades is different. Rock singer Joe Jackson thinks he knows why:

> When you get to know what a particular kind of music is all about, you realize that once in a while someone comes along who is not just working within the confines of the style but is branching out and doing something of universal interest. That's Rubén.[39]

Today salsa is heard and enjoyed all over the world. There is even an all-Japanese salsa band called Orquesta De La Luz. All the members of the band were born, raised, and live in Japan and cannot speak Spanish. They pronounce the lyrics phonetically and to the astonishment of many salsa admirers, they sound like the real thing.

Blades has been recognized by the North American music community for his achievements. He is a three-time Grammy Award winner. The first was presented to him in 1987 for his album *Escenas*. In 1988 he received his second Grammy for *Antecedente* and in 1997 his third for *La Rosa de los Vientos*. Blades commented:

> I want to be able to play anything and reach anyone. Even audiences who don't speak Spanish seem to understand the origin of the word, the honesty of our intention: to present music not as a form of entertainment that escapes reality, but as one that confronts it.[40]

Peter Manuel, a professor of music who has written about salsa, claims that most salseros would identify Rubén Blades as "the single most distinguished figure in the field."[41] Blades has also been compared to Bob Dylan, John Lennon, and Paul McCartney—three singers, songwriters, and musicians who gained enormous popularity during the 1960s.

Enrique Fernández, a Latin music critic, said of Blades,

> Like Dylan, Lennon, and McCartney, who composed literary pop music that reached a large

mass of newly educated people, Blades has fans among university students and the educated who listen because it satisfies their literary side. His appeal is broader than among those who normally would follow salsa.[42]

Blades is modest, calling himself a "people's poet" and simply saying that "I tell stories I see are not being presented. I feel if it's interesting to me as a human being, it will be interesting to other human beings."[43]

HOLLYWOOD CALLS

Rubén Blades always insists that acting is merely a way to help pay for his musical career.[1] Even still, the salsa musician has enjoyed noteworthy success in Hollywood. Since the time he watched movies in the Teatro Edison in Panama City as a boy, Blades has always been fascinated with the silver screen. In 1981 he had an opportunity to try his hand at acting. Although *The Last Fight*, a film about a down-and-out boxer's life, was a box office failure, it encouraged Blades to pursue the development of his theatrical skills.

When he first started acting, Blades's thoughts were also on events happening in his homeland. He kept in touch by traveling there two or three times a year and by reading. He was convinced that he was going to be involved politically in the future of Panama. That is when he decided that he should continue his education by earning a graduate degree in international law.

Even though he wanted to continue his education, he was becoming increasingly in demand. Blades lamented in an interview, "Once I had a lot of time and no money to pursue an education in the States. Now I have the money and it seems like I don't have enough time."[2] He explained that when he ran for political office, "I don't want people to say 'What does this guy know? He's been singing.' "[3] So he applied to one of the nation's best law schools, Harvard University in Massachusetts. He insists, however, that he did not want to go there simply to be validated by a United States institution. He wanted to learn and grow and be in a better position to become involved in his country's political future.[4] Blades already had degrees that would enable him to practice law in New York and Panama. His studies at Harvard Law School would give him an advanced degree in international law.

In 1984 he received notification that he had been admitted. He informed his family, friends, and fellow musicians that he would be taking a year off to complete the program. At the time he told a reporter:

I'm looking forward to my studies as a change of pace. You can become a little complacent [too at ease] in your own field, just from being too close to it. Besides, I want to be known as something besides a performer when I finally return to Panama, where I was born and grew up. I took a law degree there before leaving to come to New York more than ten years ago. But these additional studies will help me to specialize in international law.[5]

In the fall of 1984 he moved to Cambridge, Massachusetts, to begin his studies.

At first Blades was filled with self-doubt. He kept asking himself: "What am I doing here? What am I trying to prove? Am I trying to legitimize myself with this? Am I an arrogant idiot?" He admits that sometimes he was scared and felt like crying.[6]

Yet Blades persisted. Although his courses were difficult and he had never studied in English, Blades was a hard-working student and did well on all his assignments. He eventually met other Latinos who were studying and teaching there and enjoyed an occasional night of socializing.

During this time, he also was committed to working on another project. A small filmmaking company by the name of Max Mambru had contracted Blades to make a film called *Crossover Dreams*. *Crossover Dreams* was a low-budget but popular movie in which Blades plays a small-time salsa singer from East Harlem named Rudy Veloz. Rudy longs to "cross over" into the mainstream market of American pop music and make it big. To succeed he abandons his friends and culture. When he fails to make it to the top, he realizes that he does not have anything left. The movie's main message is that, for many people, "crossing over" means wanting to see what is on the other side. Unfortunately, people sometimes forget the culture, people, and place they left behind. Blades argues, "You don't have to leave your background behind in order to see what's on the other side."[7]

Blades was especially proud of the fact that the movie was made entirely by Latinos.[8] On a shoestring budget of only $600,000, the film was shot in sixty-two New York locations. The citizens of East Harlem allowed the crew to film in their households and even brought them soup. In exchange, the crew painted their homes. Blades marveled that "Everybody in the community cooperated. It was a Latin effort done by ourselves to help ourselves."[9]

Blades cowrote the screenplay and acted and sang in the leading part as well. His contributions to the film showed what a multitalented person he is. A movie critic said that Blades is a "screen natural" and that he is "the kind of actor whose presence and intelligence register without apparent effort."[10]

As soon as he finished the film, Blades concentrated on finishing his master's thesis. To complete his degree, Blades had to compose a lengthy essay on some aspect of international law. He chose to write about the future political development of Panama, basing his thoughts on many of the concepts and theories he had studied about at Harvard. The thesis was well accepted and on June 6, 1985, he received his degree.

Blades's interest in international affairs was not limited to his native country of Panama, however. In 1986 he collaborated with other musicians to produce a music video called *Sun City*. The project was the brainchild of Steven Van Zandt, a member of Bruce Springsteen's E-Street Band, who wanted to bring attention to the unfair policy in South Africa known as *apartheid*. Under apartheid, native black South Africans were treated as second-class citizens, had to live under restrictive and unjust laws, and were often the victims of human rights violations. Van Zandt organized musicians of all types into a group called Artists United Against Apartheid. Diverse singers and songwriters such as Bono of the Irish band U2, Bruce Springsteen, blues singer Bonnie Raitt, alternative rocker Lou Reed, funk musician George Clinton, and the rap group Run-DMC all appeared on the video, along with Blades. Their song and music video debuted on MTV in 1988.

That same year Blades appeared in *The Milagro Beanfield War*. The movie is about a small New Mexican village that is threatened by land development.

Blades was chosen for the part over two thousand other actors. He was widely praised for his part as Sheriff Bernie, who tries to keep the peace between the Anglos and the villagers. Blades said that he immediately sympathized with Sheriff Bernie, adding that he was "the man in the middle trying to avoid an explosion. In the end he takes a stand, as we all must."[11]

The film was not without critics, however, who complained that it was inappropriate for an Anglo (Robert Redford) to direct an essentially Latino film. Blades defended Redford by saying:

> No doubt there's a need for Latinos to write screenplays and for Latinos to direct. But we should try to establish collaborations with the Anglo representatives of the arts. . . . With this movie he [Redford] proves that hearts don't require visas and emotions don't require subtitles.[12]

In 1989 Blades played the role of a convicted murderer in the HBO movie *Dead Man Out*. He performed opposite Danny Glover, an accomplished actor, but critics felt that Blades's acting was superior.[13] Similarly his portrayal of a police officer in *Color of Night* led one admiring film critic to say that his fresh spin on this stock character caused him to steal every scene he was in.[14] In 1990 he was recognized for his excellent dramatic performance in *Dead Man Out* with an ACE Award.

Blades does not always play traditional Hispanic roles. In *The Two Jakes* (the sequel to *Chinatown*), for example, his character is Jewish. Jack Nicholson, the star and director of the movie, adjusted the shooting of the movie around Blades's music tour schedule. Blades appreciated the opportunity, saying "I'm sure somebody must have said, 'Jack, there are a lot of Jews in Hollywood that need a job, why are you going to a Panamanian?'"[15] Nicholson expressed his admiration for Blades, saying, "He brought a lot of energy and good acting instincts to the role. I think the result is fabulous."[16]

In 1991 the actor-director Spike Lee selected Blades to play Petey, the bookie in *Mo' Better Blues*. Lee said of his decision, "I look for people who are natural in front of the camera. Rubén is a very naturalistic actor and a really nice guy."[17]

The same year Blades appeared in another movie called *Crazy From the Heart*. In this film he starred opposite Christine Lahti in a mostly romantic comedy that also made several serious statements about prejudice. Blades plays the part of Ernesto Ontiveros, a wise Mexican-American farmer who is working as a school janitor to pay off the debt on the family ranch. He eventually wins the heart of Charlotte Bain (Lahti), the conservative school principal. The film explores the obstacles that bigotry places on people and their relationships.

Among his many acting roles, Blades starred in a movie called *Crazy From the Heart*, opposite actress Christine Lahti.

Blades's acting ability has not been overlooked. In addition to the ACE Award, he received an Emmy Award nomination for his role in *The Josephine Baker Story*. Josephine Baker was an African-American dancer who gained international acclaim in the 1920s and 1930s through her performances in Paris and New York. Blades plays Pepito Abatino, her manager and lover. Movie critics praised Blades's portrayal of Abatino.[18]

Despite his excellent acting ability, Blades has had a hard time finding quality, suitable roles. For example, when the hit TV series *Miami Vice* was on the air, Blades was asked to play the role of a drug dealer. He rejected the offer, angrily asking, "When are we going to stop playing the drug addict, the pimp, and the whore?"[19] Blades has said that "I could never do that stuff. I'd rather kill myself first."[20] Over the course of one six-month period, Blades read fifteen scripts for different shows; he was dismayed at the roles available to him. "In half, they want me to play a Colombian coke dealer. In the other half, they want me to play a Cuban coke dealer. Doesn't anybody want me to play a *lawyer*?"[21] Blades has even written on the subject, publishing an article in *The New York Times* telling the history of the negative portrayal of Latinos in American films.[22] He laments that Latinos do not always have an opportunity to dispel misconceptions.

> The truth is, in this country we Latins do not yet
> have the forum—on radio or TV or on the
> national level—to destroy stereotypes. Not
> everybody gets to play Carnegie Hall. So you can
> bet that I'm gonna try to transmit at least the
> possibility that we are different from what people
> expect.[23]

Blades's strong conviction about not reinforcing Hispanic stereotypes led him to accept the leading role in *Miracle on I-880*, a made-for-TV movie about the 1989 earthquake in San Francisco. At first he thought that the movie was going to focus on disaster and special effects. Yet when he read the script, he realized that the storyline featured a stable, decent, hard-working Hispanic family. He accepted the part. Blades hoped that the film would accustom North American audiences to seeing Hispanics in nonstereotypical roles. He wanted to show people how Hispanics "have the same pain and the same emotional possibility that white, black, or Asian families have."[24] He scoffs at the thought that when some people think of Latinos they think, "Oh, Latins, women walk around with fruit on their heads, and their men yell *olé* and have long mustaches. Why? Why does it have to be like that?"[25]

Even though Blades has acted in several TV films and programs, he feels strongly that TV does not always have a positive impact on people. At a Harvard conference on the future of TV, Blades declared: "We run the risk of being the best-informed society that ever died of ignorance. We should blame ourselves for looking at mindless things; it's a lack of respect for the intellect."[26]

Recently, Blades has appeared on Public Television's *Storytime*. In this half-hour show, Blades plays the role of Tío Rubén (Uncle Rubén). The episode is unusual because it is bilingual. In Spanish he reads *La Gallinita Roja* ("The Little Red Chicken") and *¿Dónde Está Mi Osito?* ("Where is My Little Bear?").

In 1997 Blades appeared in *The Devil's Own*, a film set in New York City and starring Harrison Ford and Brad Pitt. That same year he finished filming another movie, *Chinese Box*, in Hong Kong alongside Jeremy Irons. While acting may not be his number one priority, it is clear that Blades will continue to have a very successful career on the silver screen and in TV.

PAPA EGORÓ

The year was 1991. Blades had never lost his interest in politics. In fact, all his efforts up to that point—in film, music, and writing—stressed his concern with politics and social conditions. He closely followed events in his homeland of Panama and wrote frequent articles in the local newspapers, such as *La Estrella de Panama,*[1] as well as political essays in United States newspapers such as *The New York Times.*[2]

So it was not surprising to those closest to him that Blades formally announced his intentions of beginning a political career in Panama. His friend of twenty years Paula Campbell said, "I have seen him cry, and I have seen him depressed and desperate at seeing the condition of his people in Panama."[3] His agent Nick Stevens said, "I've always known that Rubén was interested in helping his homeland and his people above and beyond anything he was doing in the entertainment business. I always thought [the candidacy] was inevitable [certain] on some level."[4]

Blades had always kept in touch with what was happening in his home country, visiting Panama two or three times a year, although it had been almost twenty years since he had lived there. Many of his songs made reference to political issues and expressed his outrage at human rights violations throughout Latin America. The master's degree in international law that he earned from Harvard University also served to strengthen his understanding of issues. In many interviews, Blades indicated that he was interested in pursuing a life in politics. In one 1984 interview he said that "Once I go into politics, I'm not going to run for governor. I'm going to go for the whole thing."[5]

In 1991 he traveled to Panama and founded *Movimiento Papa Egoró*, which roughly translates as "Mother Earth Party" or "Motherland Party." The name was taken from the language of the local Choco Indians, Embera. The party's platform included a variety of social programs, a more equal distribution of wealth, concern for the ecology, and also supported business and private enterprise to create jobs for people. In an interview with the *Los Angeles Times*, Blades declared that Papa Egoró didn't "think or act as a traditional party. Papa Egoró vows to fight unemployment, hunger, and drugs by seeking solutions directly from the people."[6] One journalist noted that "for much of his adult life, Blades has sung about downtrodden people. Now he is trying to do something for them."[7]

Blades did not think of himself as a savior. Still, he did believe that he had some unusual qualities that might enable him to help his country:

> What I have is a strange combination of credentials that permit me to sit people down at the same table who would not ordinarily talk to each other. In Panama today there is a deep cynicism [distrust] about the Government and a sense that nothing anyone can do will make a difference. Because the young people look up to me, I believe I can stimulate them to try to address the issues and try to resolve them without expecting miracles.[8]

Blades wrote and recorded the Papa Egoró campaign theme song "The Good Seed." The song's main message is "change is coming." The party gave away free T-shirts that featured crossed maracas and the slogan "The Sound of Triumph." The campaign especially appealed to young people and others who wanted a change. In fact, Blades was quoted as saying, "If there was a kids' vote, we'd win for sure."[9]

On November 8, 1993, Panama's Elections Tribunal officially opened the campaign for the May 1994 election. The election was the first since the United States invasion in 1989 and the first free election in twenty-five years, when Arnulfo Arias was elected president of Panama in 1968. There were eighteen candidates who registered for the 1994 presidential election.

On November 28, 1993, Papa Egoró officially nominated Blades to run in the upcoming presidential election. Blades accepted the nomination to run for president of Panama. When *La Prensa*, a Panamanian newspaper, conducted an early poll, it reported that most respondents thought Blades would be Panama's next president.[10]

There were two other major candidates. One was Rubén Carles, the comptroller in the previous government. It was Ernesto Pérez Balladares, though, who was the serious challenger to Blades. Balladares belonged to the party of the former dictator of Panama, Manuel Antonio Noriega.

Blades tried to include as much of the Panamanian population in his political planning as possible. In one interview he assured the voters that "We work by consensus. I believe that the worst error that we could commit would be not to have the support of all sectors of Panamanian society."[11] For example, he made sure that Papa Egoró set aside at least half of the seats for women. "We want to make sure we ask everybody for opinions on how to solve the country's problems, including children," Blades declared.[12]

Early campaign polls showed that Blades was the "runaway favorite" to win the election.[13] Yet as the election date of May 8, 1994, neared, a poll in the Panamanian newspaper *La Prensa* showed that Blades was supported by 25 percent of the people, and Ernesto Pérez Balladares was supported by 28 percent.[14]

Ernesto Pérez Balladares was a candidate of the Revolutionary Democratic Party, the political party of General Manuel Antonio Noriega. Many felt that Balladares's association with Noriega would be the greatest danger to his election. Even still, Balladares, whose nickname was *El Toro* ("The Bull") because of his thick neck and large build, had a significant following. He promised that he would "close the Noriega chapter" in Panama's history.[15] He made many public appearances and introduced several expensive campaigns.

From the beginning there were some glaring differences in Blades's and Balladares's campaigns. While Blades's campaign fund had less than $100,[16] Balladares was a multimillionaire businessman with a well-funded political party behind him. One reporter described how the campaign offices of the Revolutionary Democratic Party were "bustling [and] air-conditioned" while Papa

Egoró's headquarters were "dusty and sparsely [barely] furnished."[17]

Some Panamanian citizens were not sure how serious or committed Blades was to politics. One woman said: "We like him, but we are not sure how serious this is. A campaign for President is not like a concert, where you just sell tickets and everyone shows up."[18] One cartoon in the local press illustrated him as a pair of maracas,[19] probably a comment on the party's logo and Blades's musical background.

Many were also concerned about Blades not having lived in Panama for the previous eighteen years. Perhaps they imagined him in the United States living the life of a movie star. How would he be able to understand their problems? The Panamanian boxing champion Roberto Durán called Blades a "scoundrel" and criticized him for not being in Panama during its most difficult moment, the 1989 United States invasion to remove Noriega.[20]

Blades and the Papa Egoró Movement were also the victims of several rumors. "I have been accused of being a CIA agent, a communist, of wanting to change the currency, of being on the military payroll, of using drugs. All of this is false," Blades said.[21] When he was challenged by rival candidate Balladares to a urine test to detect drug usage, Blades accepted and passed. He also declared that he would be willing to take a test that could detect drug usage over the last ten years.[22]

Other Panamanian citizens were concerned with the low profile the party and Blades were keeping. Some analysts feel that Blades's failure to make many public appearances wore away early support.[23] Eddy Pelletier, a citizen of Panama, complained, "I listen to all the news on TV and radio, and I haven't heard a thing [about the Blades campaign]. And there are a bunch of people like me."[24] Blades responded by saying, "I refuse to do what other politicians do, which is to barge into neighborhoods they have never been to before with TV crews and sycophants [flatterers] in tow to prove that they are men of the people."[25]

While his opponents traveled from city to city in their air-conditioned cars, Blades often hit the campaign trail on foot. One time, he walked into a poor village called Chepo on a hot and windy afternoon. As the group got larger and larger, Blades accidently stepped on a little girl's sandal and broke the strap. He knelt down, looked into her eyes, and earnestly promised her that he would replace it. When the group reached the town center, Blades vanished into a drugstore and appeared minutes later with a brand new pair of sandals for the now-content little girl.[26]

Blades also responded to the criticism of being too silent. "Our silence is the silence of he who is studying and writing. . . . What has always gone on here is superficial politicking. People who have never entered a certain neighborhood are suddenly there, with a knot of people, with flags and giving away things."[27]

The 1994 election was a first for Panama in that it had its first ever televised public debate. Four of the presidential candidates, including Blades, discussed political issues before a TV audience. According to a poll taken by *La Prensa*, Blades won the debate.[28] One political analyst argued that he was "the only candidate that presented a coherent governmental program."[29]

Blades's musical background also had an impact on the elections in that never before had TV and radio campaigns been so filled with jingles and tunes. Omaira Correa, who ran for mayor of Panama City at the same time, said that an election in Panama "has never been so musical."[30] Balladares's campaign, not to be outdone, featured a song with a catchy conga beat. Some writers even took to calling the event "the salsa elections."[31]

As May 8 neared, Blades made more personal appearances, shaking hands, providing free salsa concerts, and attending Earth Day celebrations. The day before the election, the *Miami Herald* printed an article with the headline "Too Close to Call."[32] To make sure that the election would be conducted fairly and honestly, Oliver Stone, Jesse Jackson, and former United States President Jimmy Carter were invited as observers. Later, Carter said at a news conference,

This photograph was taken of Rubén Blades during his run for the presidency of Panama in 1994.

"about 30 of us decided that we have never in our lives seen an election so perfect as this one just held in Panama."[33] The election enjoyed one of the best voter turnouts in Panamanian history; 74 percent of those eligible voted.[34]

Official results say that from among seven candidates, Blades placed third, but Blades thinks he really came in second.[35] When asked about how poor peasants could support a multimillionaire such as Pérez Balladares, Blades asserts his belief that most people do not believe that change is possible. So they support the person or party who seems to be strongest or to have more political pull.[36] Balladares will be president of Panama from 1994 to 1999. Even though Blades did not win the election, Papa Egoró, the party he started, now has at least seven representatives in the government.

In 1994 the Panamanian legislature formally approved the abolition of its armed forces. After the 1989 removal of Manuel Noriega, the new government replaced the Panamanian Army with the civilian organization, the Public Force. The United States began discussions with Panama to have the United States Army installed there. Blades is opposed to the United States maintaining a military presence in Panama. Blades has said, "It seems contradictory to me that Panama rejects its own armed forces but accepts another country's armed forces."[37] He firmly believes that Panamanians do not want to become the "51st state" of the United States.[38]

At noon on December 31, 1999, the Panama Canal and United States military bases will be returned to Panama. This transfer was agreed upon in the Carter-Torrijos Canal Treaty of 1977. Many Panamanians were upset that, at the treaty signing, not one Panamanian was present to represent the country. Nonetheless, surveys indicate that 70 percent of Panamanians oppose the withdrawal of United States troops, which will bring unemployment to about 6,000 Panamanians who currently work for United States businesses within the Canal Zone.[39] Placing the Canal Zone and all the other United States holdings under complete Panamanian control will undoubtedly have a significant impact on the country.

Blades has told his concert audiences that he is trying to shape a third position in the politics of Latin America, neither right nor left, but one that will create a stronger, more unified Latin America. He explains, "What I propose is to create what up to this point has been a mythical place: a Latin America that respects and loves itself, is incorruptible, romantic, nationalistic, and has a human perception of the needs of the world at large."[40] All of Blades's work—in singing, acting, and in politics—underscores that goal.

Blades continues to follow local developments in Panama. He still enjoys enormous popularity in his homeland. A spokesperson for the Panamanian consulate once said, "We just love him. He's like a roving ambassador for Panama."[41] His determination to have an impact on the political life of Panama remains strong, and he has vowed on many occasions that he will return to his homeland permanently. "My life is a cycle that began in Panama, and it will close there."[42]

TODAY AND
TOMORROW

Rubén Blades's music has influenced bands all over the world. In Cuba the popular group Los Van Van recorded "Tierra Dura" ("Hard Land"), a song about Ethiopia arranged by Blades.[1] Juan Formel, the band's leader, also adopted the trap drum set into his group, as Blades had done. Blades feels that his greatest contribution has been the emergence of a "new attitude." He believes that young musicians are more aware of their responsibility: "They seem to understand the need to be educated, the perils of drug use, the necessity to conduct themselves in a responsible way."[2] He also serves as a model to young musicians to explore other forms of artistry—film, TV, and theater.

Yet perhaps where Blades has had the most impact has been in his songwriting and lyrics. "Before me," he says, "no one wrote songs that went beyond the traditional short song with a mambo chorus as a way to escape reality, or wrote lyrics that treated issues dealing with life."[3] Music critics agree, saying that he made his mark in salsa with literate, socially conscious lyrics.

Blades continues to write music that informs about social conditions and that motivates people to reflect. As he says, "I do have an obligation to myself to be of consequence. I know the streets well, and it worries me a lot what I see because I do not see hope in certain faces. It doesn't depress me. It inspires me."[4] He takes his commitment seriously, saying:

> In Latin America we don't have too many heroes, so musicians carry a heavy responsibility. I'm very much concerned about the young people who listen to our music. But I don't ask myself if music is going to change things. I ask only whether my music will make somebody ask something—put a question into a kid's mind that might otherwise not have been there.[5]

Blades continues to dream of a world community where people can appreciate all cultures. He looks to a "society that will be more integrated and fair, where character will be the most important thing, where hearts don't require visas."[6] Blades laments, "We have lost our sense of justice, of wanting to do things for each other."[7] In his song "Muévete" ("Move On"), he laments that "most of us seek our own comfort . . . those who go up front seldom look back to help those in need." He concludes by asking all of us, from "the Caribbean to Soweto in Africa," to work together for a better future for all.

At a concert in Washington, D.C.'s Kennedy Center in 1987, he asked the audience for its support:

> I'm going to ask a favor. I'm going to speak in English tonight, but don't accuse me of selling out or anything. These people [English-only speakers] came here to share our culture with us, and this will help them understand what we're trying to do.[8]

Blades is sensitive to critics who feel he has "sold out." Some critics claim that when he moved to Hollywood in 1987 and married Lisa Lebenzon, a blond, blue-eyed North American actress, he "crossed over" to the other side. Some even feel that Lebenzon might have been a disadvantage in his bid for the Panamanian presidential election. Leon Ichaso, the director of *Crossover Dreams*, has said, "Deep down, he [Blades] knows he's forgotten his friends, his people, his country, his music, and himself."[9]

Many others, however, defend Blades. "Blades is not crossing over *to* a new audience so much as he is crossing over *with* a new audience."[10] After all, some would argue that the Latino culture both inside and outside of the United States is becoming increasingly Anglo. Blades explains that he finds "the whole idea of crossover dangerous, because it implies the abandonment of one base for another. I'd rather talk about convergence—the idea of two sides meeting in the middle of a bridge."[11]

His album *Nothing But the Truth* was hailed as an attempt to cross over to a wider, "whiter" audience, but Blades disagrees. He says that the album was "more like a 'meet halfway.' People can relate to any music on earth provided they have a shot at listening to it."[12] This is very reminiscent of his boyhood inspiration, Piero, who felt that people cannot appreciate music if they are not ever exposed to it.[13]

Although Blades is sorry he had to turn down playing the part of Brazilian environmentalist Chico Mendes, he has already received other film and TV offers. He is working on a new TV series called *Falls Road*. *Falls Road* is very different from most family dramas in that the central character, detective Luis Juega (played by Blades) is Latino. The actor likes the fact that Juega's culture almost becomes secondary to the part: "I thought that was very intriguing. I would be more of a person."[14]

Blades keeps modest homes in cities he visits often—Los Angeles, New York City, and Panama

City—although he spends most of his time in California and Panama. Interestingly, he does not own a car or have a driver's license. Although he says that someday that will happen, he has other priorities to contend with.

Of his wife Lisa Lebenzon, Blades has said, "We are good friends."[15] She is an actress and lives most of the time in California. Before Blades married Lisa Lebenzon, he asked her to learn to speak Spanish so that they could converse at home in his native language. Not only did she agree to do so, but she finished a three-year Spanish language course in just seven months.[16]

"We are very private people," Blades has said of their home life. "We read a lot. We don't go out much. You know, our dog, flowers in the garden, the whole thing."[17] Library shelves hold books by Albert Camus, Franz Kafka, George Orwell, Ernest Hemingway, Gabriel García Márquez, Groucho Marx, and Woody Allen. There is also a collection of *Mad* and *National Lampoon* magazines.[18] But whereas he favored fiction as a youth, as an adult, Blades prefers nonfiction works—books that deal with current situations or historical events. Sometimes Blades likes to unwind by painting watercolors.

One of Blades's hobbies is cooking, especially for friends. His favorite foods are based on spending countless hours watching his grandmother in the kitchen. One of his beloved recipes is a flavorful black bean dish he serves with rice and plantains (a kind of banana that must be cooked before eaten). Blades points out that beans are full of protein and claims to have tried black beans "in every restaurant you can imagine."[19]

One of the things that has helped Blades be so successful overall is the fact that he never got involved with drugs. "If I had been into drugs, I would never have been able to face the consequences of my work or the expectations of other people."[20] But he is cautious about defining success. Blades was once asked to provide *his* definition of success, but he hesitated, stating:

> I did not feel that I could really define it, not only because it was such a subjective issue, but also because some of the most inspirational events in human history came as a result of alleged failures. The two examples that come immediately to mind are the life of Jesus Christ and Dunkirk [the World War II British troop defeat and evacuation from which Great Britain learned from its mistakes and eventually was on the winning side]. From those two events, tremendous lessons were learned. However, I can define failure: failure is not to try.[21]

Blades urges young people to concentrate on their studies. He considers education "an intellectual .45 [gun] you can carry with you."[22] He points out that one's education is something that no one can take away. "No one is going to bury you with your BMW; but your integrity and your education—those are with you always." Blades continues his education in his spare time, reading up on a variety of topics and studying and practicing other languages. He is fluent in English and Spanish and has an understanding of French and Portuguese. His goal is to speak four or five languages.[23]

Ever since the 1994 Panamanian election, Blades has concentrated on his life and career as an artist. While he was campaigning (1993–1994) he did not work, so he has focused on his music and acting since then. He chooses his projects and his roles carefully, not wishing to perpetuate Latino stereotypes.

> In the States right now I have a good opportunity to dispel some of the myths about Latin Americans in this country, the stereotypes that were really created by the entertainment industry. The woman with the fruit on her head, the bum, the drug addict, and the lowlife. All of that I can help change because I don't fit any of those categories.[24]

Blades believes that Latinos need to be more attentive to opportunities to change these images.

> We Latins have got only ourselves to change the stereotypes. We've got to show the intelligent side of the Latin American. So that's what I try to present musically and culturally in the lyrics—but in no way do I think that's going to get me to Las

Vegas, and I'm not interested at all to play Las
Vegas.[25]

Blades declares that "I will never be a superstar. My
role is to be different, to do what others won't do, and,
as a result, my fortunes will always fluctuate. I will
always be viewed with suspicion by some, though not
by all, because I move against the current."[26]

For now Blades is content to write his music, sing
his songs, and portray suitable characters on film and
TV. His latest album, *La Rosa de los Vientos,* was
recorded in his native Panama with over twenty-five
Panamanian musicians. It includes contemporary
salsa, traditional Latin American music, Panamanian
folk music, rock music, and slow and romantic *boleros.*
For this work, Blades received his third Grammy
Award in 1997.

Although Blades knew he had been nominated for
a Grammy in the category of "Tropical Latin," he was
not able to attend the awards ceremony because he
was wrapping up the filming of *Chinese Box* with
Jeremy Irons. As he flew from Hong Kong to Puerto
Rico for a concert engagement, he was given the good
news. Soon after landing in San Juan he was interviewed from his hotel. He said: "Awards are always
difficult because someone always wins and others lose.
And I think that no one should have to lose." In that
interview, the singer went on to explain why his third
Grammy was especially significant to him: *"La Rosa de*

In addition to singing and acting, Rubén Blades takes on activities like reading to children on the PBS series *Storytime*.

los Vientos has been a work made entirely in Panama. And for me this Grammy has been a validation of the quality of artistic talent in Panama."[27]

For his next album, the singer promises to steer away from traditional salsa and to explore a new musical style that he calls *panamerican*. He envisions a new genre that would merge musical elements from South America, North America, and the Caribbean. Says the singer, "After having been in the vanguard [forefront] of salsa for so many years, now I want to go in another direction."[28]

One of the new directions Blades will pursue is acting. After receiving so many favorable reviews for his film work, Blades learned that he is going to be honored with a star on Hollywood's Walk of Fame. In 1998 a star with Blades's name on it will be added to the famous sidewalk. Other recipients will include musician Kenny G. and actors Nicholas Cage, Bruce Willis, and Joe Pesci. Blades was the only Latino selected for the honor that year.[29]

Blades acknowledges: "I do have my own definition of *happiness* and I realize that I am happy more often than not—no matter how difficult or desperate the situation seems to be."[30] For the many who find themselves in exactly those kinds of discouraging conditions, Rubén Blades's work will continue to be a source of inspiration and hope for years to come.

Chronology

1948—Rubén Blades is born in Panama City, Panama, on July 16.

1964—Panama Canal Zone riots.

1968—Blades begins his studies at the University of Panama and makes an album with Bush and the Magnificos in Panama; Panamanian President Arias is overthrown in a military coup; Colonel Omar Torrijos eventually assumes control.

1969—Blades travels to New York.

1970—*De Panamá a Nueva York: Pete Rodríguez Presenta a Rubén Blades,* Blades's first album, is recorded.

1972—Blades graduates with a law degree from the University of Panama.

1974—Blades debuts at Madison Square Garden with Ray Barretto's band.

1976—Blades begins collaboration with Willie Colón.

1977—Blades and Colón produce *Willie Colón Presents Rubén Blades.*

1978—Colón and Blades release *Siembra,* the most popular salsa album in history.

1981—After Torrijos is killed in a plane crash, General Manuel Noriega assumes leadership of Panama; Blades makes acting debut in *The Last Fight.*

1982—Blades officially breaks with Willie Colón and starts his own band called Seis del Solar.

1984—Blades is the first salsero signed by a mainstream label (Elektra/Asylum); Releases *Buscando América;* Moves to Cambridge to attend Harvard University's Law School.

1985—*Escenas* is released; Blades stars in *Crossover Dreams*; Blades meets Nobel Prize–winning author Gabriel García Márquez; Earns master's degree in international law from Harvard University.

1986—Debuts at Carnegie Hall; Appears in the anti-apartheid music video *Sun City.*

1987—*Agua de Luna* is released; Wins Grammy Award for *Escenas;* Moves to Los Angeles; Marries Lisa Lebenzon.

1988—Blades's first record in English, *Nothing But the Truth,* is released; Receives his second Grammy Award for *Antecedente;* Appears in *The Milagro Beanfield War.*

1989—Seis del Solar becomes known as Son del Solar; Noriega is overthrown by a United States invasion; *Antecedente* is released; Blades plays role of a convicted murderer in *Dead Man Out;* Has leading role in *Miracle on I-880.*

1990—Receives ACE Award for *Dead Man Out;* Appears in *The Two Jakes* and *Predator 2.*

1991—Appears in *Mo' Better Blues* and *The Super;* Stars opposite Christine Lahti in *Crazy From the Heart; Caminando* is released; Founds political party "Movimiento Papa Egoró."

1993—*Amor y Control* is released; Papa Egoró officially nominates Blades to run in the upcoming Panamanian presidential election.

1994—Loses election to Ernesto Pérez Balladares.

1996—Records *La Rosa de Los Vientos;* Continues his songwriting, singing, and acting.

1997—Receives third Grammy for *La Rosa de los Vientos;* Appears in *The Devil's Own* alongside Harrison Ford and Brad Pitt; Wraps up filming of *Chinese Box* in Hong Kong.

SELECTED FILMS, SOUND RECORDINGS, AND TV PROGRAMS

SOUND RECORDINGS

Willie Colón Presents Rubén Blades (1977)

Siembra (1978)—with Willie Colón

Bohemio y Poeta (1979)

Maestra Vida (1980)

Canciones del Solar de los Aburridos (1981) —with Willie Colón

Mucho Mejor (1984)

Buscando América (1984)

Crossover Dreams— soundtrack (1985)

Rubén Blades y Seis del Solar (1985)

Escenas (1985)

Sun City (1986)

Agua de Luna (1987)

Nothing But the Truth (1988)

Antecedente (1989)

Caminando (1991)

Amor y Control (1993)

Tras la Tormenta (1996) —with Willie Colón

La Rosa de los Vientos (1996)

FILMS

The Last Fight (1983)

Crossover Dreams (1985)

Critical Condition (1986)

Fatal Beauty (1987)

Salsa: Latin Music of New York and Puerto Rico (1988)

The Milagro Beanfield War (1988)

Disorganized Crime (1989)

Q & A (1990)

The Two Jakes (1990)

Predator 2 (1990)

The Super (1991)

Mo' Better Blues (1991)

Color of Night (1994)

The Devil's Own (1997)

TV PROGRAMS

AIDS: Changing the Rules (1987)

Routes of Rhythm (1989)

Dead Man Out (1989)

Miracle on I-880 (1989)

One Man's War (1991)

The Josephine Baker Story (1991)

Crazy From the Heart (1991)

CHAPTER NOTES

CHAPTER 1

1. David Hershkovits, "Tuning Up," *Daily News*, July 22, 1984, p. 6.

2. Paula Span, "Rubén Blades & the Spirit of Salsa," *Washington Post*, November 5, 1985, p. B6.

3. George Priestly, *Military Government and Popular Participation in Panama* (Boulder, Colo.: Westview Press, 1986), p. 24.

4. Pete Hamill, "Hey, It's Rubén Blades," *New York*, August 19, 1985, p. 47.

5. Span, p. B6.

6. Robert A. Parker, "The Vision of Rubén Blades," *Américas*, vol. 37, no. 2, March-April 1985, p. 16.

7. Stephen Holden, "Rubén Blades Turns His Talents to Movies," *New York Times Biographical Service*, vol. 16, no. 8, August 1985, pp. 978–979.

8. Hershkovits, p. 6.

9. Stephen Holden, "Rubén Blades Turns His Talents to Movies," *The New York Times*, August 18, 1985, p. H16.

10. José Tcherkaski, *Piero* (Buenos Aires, Argentina: Editorial Galerna, 1983), p. 19.

11. Ibid., p. 27.

12. Betty A. Marton, *Rubén Blades* (New York: Chelsea House Publishers, 1992), p. 31.

CHAPTER 2

1. Pete Hamill, "Hey, It's Rubén Blades," *New York*, August 19, 1985, p. 46.

2. Jay Cocks, "The Keen Edge of Rubén Blades," *Time*, July 2, 1984, p. 82.

3. David Hershkovits, "Tuning Up," *Daily News*, July 22, 1984, p. 6.

4. Private interview with Rubén Blades, June 26, 1996.

5. Hamill, p. 46.

6. Paula Span, "Rubén Blades & the Spirit of Salsa," *Washington Post*, November 5, 1985, p. B6.

7. Jay Cocks, "Of Ghosts and Magic," *Time*, July 11, 1988, p. 52.

8. Betty A. Marton, *Rubén Blades* (New York: Chelsea House Publishers, 1992), pp. 26–27.

9. Ibid., p. 27.

10. Bill Barol, "Salsa with a Political Spin," *Newsweek*, September 9, 1985, p. 97.

11. Span, p. B6.

12. Guy D. Garcia, "Salsa: Rubén Blades," *Interview*, April 1986, p. 210.

13. Hamill, p. 47.

14. Marton, p. 28.

15. Stephen Holden, "Rubén Blades Turns His Talents to Movies," *New York Times Biographical Service*, August 1985, p. 978.

16. Span, p. B6.

17. Marton, p. 25.

18. Hamill, p. 47.

19. Robert Blau, "Singer Rubén Blades Goes from Salsa to Cinema in *Crossover Dreams*," *Chicago Tribune*, October 6, 1985, p. 16, Section 13.

20. Span, p. B6.

21. Hershkovits, p. 6.

22. John Morthland, "Outgrowing Salsa, Searching for America," *Newsday*, April 22, 1984, p. 27.

CHAPTER 3

1. Stephen Holden, "Rubén Blades Turns His Talents to Movies," *The New York Times*, August 18, 1985, p. H16.

2. Betty A. Marton, *Rubén Blades* (New York: Chelsea House Publishers, 1992), p. 34.

3. Private interview, June 26, 1996.

4. Thomas E. Skidmore and Peter H. Smith, *Modern Latin America* (New York: Oxford University Press, 1989), pp. 315–316.

5. Carlos Guevara Mann, *Panamanian Militarism: A Historical Interpretation* (Athens, Ohio: Ohio University Center for International Studies, 1996), p. 93.

6. Omar Torrijos Herrera, *La Batalla de Panamá* as quoted in George Priestly, *Military Government and Popular Participation in Panama* (Boulder, Colo.: Westview Press, 1986), p. 31.

7. Jeremy Marre and Hannah Charlton, *Beats of the Heart: Popular Music of the World* (New York: Pantheon Books, 1985), p. 70.

8. Peter Manuel, *Caribbean Currents: Caribbean Music from Rumba to Reggae* (Philadelphia, Pa.: Temple University Press, 1995), p. 73.

9. Frank M. Figueroa, *Encyclopedia of Latin American Music in New York* (St. Petersburg, Fla.: Pillar Publications, 1994), p. 153.

10. Achy Obejas, "Rubén Blades Gives New Meaning to *Salsa*," *Nuestro*, April 1984, p. 51.

11. Tracy Wilkinson, "Rubén Blades' Panamanian Pipe Dream," *Los Angeles Times Magazine*, April 24, 1994, p. 32.

12. Robert A. Parker, "The Vision of Rubén Blades," *Américas*, vol. 37, no. 2, March-April 1985, p. 16.

13. Marton, p. 43.

CHAPTER 4

1. Stephen Holden, "Rubén Blades Turns His Talents to Movies," *New York Times Biographical Service*, vol. 16, no. 8, August 1985, p. 978.

2. Frank M. Figueroa, *Encyclopedia of Latin American Music in New York* (St. Petersburg, Fla.: Pillar Publications, 1994), p. 69.

3. Betty A. Marton, *Rubén Blades* (New York: Chelsea House Publishers, 1992), p. 47.

4. Jeremy Marre and Hannah Charlton, *Beats of the Heart: Popular Music of the World* (New York: Pantheon Books, 1985), p. 80.

5. Peter Manuel, *Caribbean Currents: Caribbean Music from Rumba to Reggae* (Philadelphia, Pa.: Temple University Press, 1995), p. 77.

6. Figueroa, p. 37.

7. Willie Colón, "The Rhythms," *The Portable Lower East Side* (New York: Grove Press, 1988), p. 11.

8. Anthony DePalma, "Rubén Blades: Up From Salsa," *New York Times Biographical Service*, vol. 18, no. 6, June 1987, p. 595.

9. Figueroa, p. 36.

10. Robert A. Parker, "The Vision of Rubén Blades," *Américas*, vol. 37, no. 2, March-April 1985, p. 17.

11. Achy Obejas, "Rubén Blades Gives New Meaning to *Salsa,*" *Nuestro*, April 1984, p. 51.

12. DePalma, p. 594.

13. Figueroa, p. 47.

14. Parker, p. 17.

15. Marton, p. 66.

16. Obejas, p. 51.

17. DePalma, p. 595.

18. Figueroa, p. 125.

19. Manuel, p. 74.

20. Armando Bermúdez, "Rubén Blades Dice que Panamá no Quiere Ser Estado 51," *Impacto Latin News*, February 2, 1993, p. 6.

21. Manuel, p. 87.

CHAPTER 5

1. Charley Gerard and Marty Sheller, *Salsa! The Rhythm of Latin Music* (Crown Point, Ind.: White Cliffs Media Co., 1989), p. 12.

2. Interview with T. M. Scruggs, professor of ethnomusicology at the University of Iowa, May 15, 1996.

3. Stephen Holden, "Rubén Blades Turns His Talents to Movies," *New York Times Biographical Service*, vol. 16, no. 8, August 1985, p. 978.

4. Richard Harrington, "Latino Lyrics," *Washington Post*, June 22, 1984, p. B4.

5. Jeremy Marre and Hannah Charlton, *Beats of the Heart: Popular Music of the World* (New York: Pantheon Books, 1985), p. 80.

6. Fred Bouchard, "Rubén Blades," *Down Beat*, vol. 53, January 1986, p. 14.

7. Jay Cocks, "Of Ghosts and Magic," *Time*, July 11, 1988, p. 52.

8. Robert Palmer, "The Pop Life: Rubén Blades's Salsa," *The New York Times*, April 4, 1984, p. C21.

9. Bill Barol, "Salsa with a Political Spin," *Newsweek*, September 9, 1985, p. 97.

10. Jan Herman, "Rubén Blades' Crowning Glory," *Daily News*, August 21, 1985, p. 45.

11. Pamela Bloom, "A Rubén Blades Close-Up," *High Fidelity*, vol. 36, April 1986, p. 75.

12. John Morthland, "Outgrowing Salsa, Searching for America," *Newsday*, April 22, 1984, p. 27.

13. Betty A. Marton, *Rubén Blades* (New York: Chelsea House Publishers, 1992), p. 63.

14. Peter Manuel, *Caribbean Currents: Caribbean Music from Rumba to Reggae* (Philadelphia, Pa.: Temple University Press, 1995), p. 82.

15. Silvana Paternostro, "After Noriega, Drugs Still Flow," *Miami Herald*, May 8, 1994, p. 5C.

16. Guy D. Garcia, "Singer, Actor, Politico," *Time*, January 29, 1990, p. 72.

17. Morthland, p. 27.

18. Rubén Blades as quoted in an interview with Fred Bouchard, *Down Beat*, January 1986, p. 14.

19. Norma Niurka, "En Radio Miami Hay Cantantes Sin Voz," *El Herald*, December 15, 1985, p. 10.

20. Paula Span, "Rubén Blades & the Spirit of Salsa," *Washington Post*, November 5, 1985, p. B6.

21. "Rubén Blades: 'Quiero el Poder'," *Impacto Latin News*. January 25, 1994, p. 15.

22. Bloom, p. 76.

23. Ibid.

24. Gerard and Sheller, p. 10.

25. Marre and Charlton, p. 80.

26. Robert A. Parker, "The Vision of Rubén Blades," *Américas*, vol. 37, no. 2, March-April 1985, p. 19.

27. Holden, p. 979.

28. Guy D. Garcia, "Salsa: Rubén Blades," *Interview*, April 1986, p. 210.

29. Harrington, p. B4.

30. Holden, p. 979.

31. Anthony DePalma, "Rubén Blades: Up From Salsa," *New York Times Biographical Service,* vol. 18, no. 6, June 1987, p. 595.

32. Achy Obejas, "Rubén Blades Gives New Meaning to *Salsa*," *Nuestro*, April 1984, p. 51.

33. Jay Cocks, "Of Ghosts and Magic," *Time*, July 11, 1988, p. 52.

34. "Rubén Blades and Son de Solar" (concert review), *Variety*, July 12, 1989, p. 93.

35. Marton, p. 41.

36. Laura Lippman, "Rubén Blades, Man of Many Roles, Plays Cop Again," *The Miami Herald*, April 6, 1996, p. 5G.

37. Garcia, 1986, p. 210.

38. Ibid.

39. Eric Levin, "A Novelist's Eye, A Humanist's Heart, and a Hot Band Make Rubén Blades' Salsa *Numero Uno*," *People's Weekly*, August 13, 1984, p. 76.

40. Bloom, p. 77.

41. Manuel, p. 79.

42. David Hershkovits, "Tuning Up," *Daily News*, July 22, 1984, p. 6.

43. Levin, p. 75.

CHAPTER 6

1. Jay Cocks, "Of Ghosts and Magic," *Time*, July 11, 1988, p. 52.

2. Richard Harrington, "Latino Lyrics," *Washington Post*, June 22, 1984, p. B4.

3. Betty A. Marton, *Rubén Blades* (New York: Chelsea House Publishers, 1992), p. 67.

4. Jan Herman, "Rubén Blades' Crowning Glory," *Daily News*, August 21, 1985, p. 45.

5. Robert Palmer, "The Pop Life: Rubén Blades's Salsa," *The New York Times*, April 4, 1984, p. C21.

6. Paula Span, "Rubén Blades & the Spirit of Salsa," *Washington Post*, November 5, 1985, p. B6.

7. Bill Barol, "Salsa with a Political Spin," *Newsweek*, September 9, 1985, p. 97.

8. Stephen Holden, "Rubén Blades Turns His Talents to Movies," *New York Times Biographical Service*, vol. 16, no. 8, August 1985, p. 979.

9. Stephen Holden, "Rubén Blades Turns His Talents to Movies," *The New York Times*, August 18, 1985, p. H16.

10. Vincent Canby, *"Crossover Dreams:* Review," *The New York Times*, August 18, 1985, p. H8.

11. Anthony DePalma, "Rubén Blades: Up From Salsa," *New York Times Biographical Service*, vol. 18, no. 6, June 1987, p. 596.

12. David Ansen, "Trouble in Miracle Valley," *Newsweek*, March 28, 1988, p. 68.

13. John Leonard, "Mental Detector," *New York*, March 13, 1989, p. 70.

14. David Small, *"Color of Night"* (review), *The New Yorker*, September 5, 1994, p. 107.

15. George Hadley-Garcia, *Hispanic Hollywood: The Latins in Motion Pictures* (New York: Carol Publishing Group, 1990), p. 232.

16. Guy D. Garcia, "Singer, Actor, Politico," *Time*, January 29, 1990, p. 70.

17. Ibid.

18. *"The Josephine Baker Story"* (review), *Variety*, March 11, 1991, p. 68.

19. DePalma, p. 596.

20. Pete Hamill, "Hey, It's Rubén Blades," *New York*, August 19, 1985, p. 44.

21. Ibid., p. 45.

22. Rubén Blades, "The Politics Behind the Latino's Legacy," *The New York Times*, April 19, 1992, p. H31.

23. Pamela Bloom, "A Rubén Blades Close-Up," *High Fidelity*, vol. 36, April 1986, p. 77.

24. Antonio Mejias-Renta, "Rubén Blades contra los estereotipos," *La Opinion*, February 22, 1993, p. 1D.

25. Robert Blau, "Singer Rubén Blades Goes from Salsa to Cinema in *Crossover Dreams*," *Chicago Tribune*, October 6, 1985, p. 16.

26. Bill Kirtz, "Top Execs Take Hard Look at TV's Future," *Broadcasting*, February 15, 1993, p. 12.

CHAPTER 7

1. Laura Lippman, "Rubén Blades, Man of Many Roles, Plays Cop Again," *Miami Herald*, April 6, 1996, p. 5G.

2. Rubén Blades, "The Politics Behind the Latino's Legacy," *The New York Times*, April 19, 1992, p. H31.

3. José Torres, "Rubén Blades: Un Verdadero Señor," *El Diario/La Prensa*, March 29, 1994, p. 17.

4. Tracy Wilkinson, "Rubén Blades' Panamanian Pipe Dream," *Los Angeles Times Magazine*, April 24, 1994, p. 30.

5. Richard Harrington, "Latino Lyrics," *Washington Post*, June 22, 1984, p. B4.

6. "Singer's Panama Platform Reveals that Santa Monica Zeal," *Los Angeles Times*, March 10, 1994, p. J2.

7. Meg Grant, "Panama's Favorite Son," *People's Weekly*, May 9, 1994, p. 181.

8. Stephen Holden, "Rubén Blades Turns His Talents to Movies," *The New York Times*, August 18, 1985, p. H16.

9. Grant, p. 181.

10. Amy Wilentz, "Slippery Blades," *The New Republic*, November 1, 1993, p. 11.

11. "Rubén Blades: 'Quiero el Poder,'" *Impacto Latin News*, January 25, 1994, p. 15.

12. "Singer's Panama Platform Reveals that Santa Monica Zeal," *Los Angeles Times*, March 10, 1994, p. J2.

13. Howard W. French, "Panama Likes Rubén Blades But Not, It Seems, as Leader," *New York Times Biographical Service*, March, 1994, p. 405.

14. "Panama Race Gets Tighter," *The New York Times*, May 2, 1994, p. A7.

15. Paul Goodwin, Jr., *Global Studies: Latin America* (Guilford, Conn.: Dushkin Publishing Group), p. 48.

16. French, p. 405.

17. Howard W. French, "Panama Journal: Democracy at Work, Under Shadow of Dictators," *The New York Times*, February 21, 1994, p. 4A.

18. Howard W. French, "Panama Likes Rubén Blades But Not, It Seems, as Leader," *New York Times Biographical Service*, March 1994, p. 405.

19. Wilkinson, p. 30.

20. Tim Johnson, "Presenting . . . The Candidates of Panama," *Miami Herald*, May 6, 1994, p. 22A.

21. Tim Johnson, "Singer's Recent Surge Makes Panama Race Too Close to Call," *Miami Herald*, May 4, 1994, p. 5A.

22. Maite Rico, "El Pipí del Candidato," *País*, May 8, 1994, p. 12.

23. Tracy Wilkinson, "Panama Reprise? Manuel Noriega's Old Party Seems Poised for Victory in Upcoming Elections," *Los Angeles Times*, March 22, 1994, p. H5.

24. Wilkinson, "Rubén Blades' Panamanian Pipe Dream," p. 30.

25. "Panama Journal: Democracy at Work, Under Shadow of Dictators," *The New York Times*, February 21, 1994, p. 4A.

26. Grant, p. 181.

27. Wilkinson, "Rubén Blades' Panamanian Pipe Dream," p. 30.

28. Juan L. Batista, "Según Sondeo: Rubén Blades Gana Debate," *La Prensa*, April 24, 1994, p. 1A.

29. Sharon Phillipps Collazos, "Politics as Usual in Panamanian Elections?" *The Christian Science Monitor*, May 5, 1994, p. 19.

30. Johnson, "Presenting . . . The Candidates of Panama," p. 22A.

31. Mariela Sagel, "Panamá: Las Elecciones de la Salsa," *El Nuevo Herald*, May 6, 1994, p. 13A.

32. Johnson, "Singer's Recent Surge Makes Panama Race Too Close to Call," p. 1A.

33. Tim Johnson, "Panama Erases Blot of '89 Fraud," *Miami Herald*, May 10, 1994, p. 7A.

34. "Proclaman a Pérez Balladares," *La Prensa*, May 12, 1994, p. 1A.

35. Lippman, p. 5G.

36. Private interview with Rubén Blades, June 26, 1996.

37. French, p. 4A.

38. Armando Bermúdez, "Rubén Blades Dice que Panamá no Quiere Ser Estado 51," *Impacto Latin News*, February 2, 1993, p. 6.

39. Amanda C. Brown-Stevens, *Mesoamerica*, vol. 13, no. 2, February 1994, p. 14.

40. Guy D. Garcia, "Singer, Actor, Politico," *Time*, January 29, 1990, p. 70.

41. David Hershkovits, "Tuning Up," *Daily News*, July 22, 1984, p. 18.

42. Wilkinson, p. 47.

CHAPTER 8

1. Charley Gerard and Marty Sheller, *Salsa! The Rhythm of Latin Music* (Crown Point, Ind.: White Cliffs Media Co., 1989), p. 7.

2. Private interview with Rubén Blades, June 26, 1996.

3. Ibid.

4. Tracy Wilkinson, "Ruben Blades' Panamanian Pipe Dream," *Los Angeles Times Magazine*, April 24, 1994, p. 30.

5. Jeremy Marre and Hannah Charlton, *Beats of the Heart: Popular Music of the World* (New York: Pantheon Books, 1985), p. 80.

6. Jay Cocks, "Of Ghosts and Magic," *Time*, July 11, 1988, p. 52.

7. Robert A. Parker, "The Vision of Rubén Blades," *Américas*, vol. 37, no. 2, March-April 1985, p. 18.

8. Anthony DePalma, "Rubén Blades: Up From Salsa," *New York Times Biographical Service*, vol. 18, no. 6, June 1987, p. 594.

9. Ibid., p. 596.

10. Don Michael Randel, "Crossing Over with Rubén Blades," *Journal of the American Musicological Society*, vol. 44, no. 2, Summer 1991, p. 322.

11. Stephen Holden, "Rubén Blades Turns His Talents to Movies," *New York Times Biographical Service*, vol. 16, no. 8, August 1985, p. 978.

12. Cocks, p. 52.

13. José Tcherkaski, *Piero* (Buenos Aires, Argentina: Editorial Galerna, 1983), p. 29.

14. Laura Lippman, "Rubén Blades, Man of Many Roles, Plays Cop Again," *Miami Herald*, April 6, 1996, p. 5G.

15. Private interview with Rubén Blades.

16. Armando Bermúdez, "Rubén Blades Dice que Panamá no Quiere Ser Estado 51," *Impacto Latin News*, February 2, 1993, p. 6.

17. Howard W. French, "Panama Likes Ruben Blades But Not, It Seems, as Leader," *The New York Times*, March 17, 1994, p. 14A.

18. Charles Moritz, ed., *Current Biography Yearbook* (New York: The H. W. Wilson Company, 1986), p. 49.

19. Michael Winerip, "A Rubén Blades Special," *The New York Times Magazine*, June 2, 1991, p. 46.

20. Parker, p. 18.

21. Private interview with Rubén Blades.

22. Paula Span, "Rubén Blades & the Spirit of Salsa," *Washington Post*, November 5, 1985, p. B6.

23. Private interview with Rubén Blades.

24. Guy D. Garcia, "Salsa: Rubén Blades," *Interview*, April 1986, p. 210.

25. John Morthland, "Outgrowing Salsa, Searching for America," *Newsday*, April 22, 1984, p. 1127.

26. Guy D. Garcia, "Singer, Actor, Politico," *Time*, January 29, 1990, p. 70.

27. Evelio Taillacq, "Salsa Para Oír y Latin Jazz Para Bailar, Ganon en los Grammy," *Exito,* March 5, 1997, p. 48.

28. "¿Se le Acabó la Salsa a Blades?" *El Nuevo Herald*, October 15, 1996, p. 2C.

29. "Rubén Blades: Una Estrella en Hollywood," *El Nuevo Herald,* June 29, 1997, p. 2B.

30. Private interview with Rubén Blades.

FURTHER READING

Bloom, Pamela. "A Rubén Blades Close-Up." *High Fidelity,* vol. 36, April 1986, 75–77.

Garcia, Guy D. "Singer, Actor, Politico." *Time,* vol. 135, no. 5, January 29, 1990, 70–73.

Hamill, Pete. "Hey, It's Rubén Blades." *New York,* August 19, 1985, 42–49.

Marton, Betty A. *Rubén Blades.* New York: Chelsea House Publishers, 1992.

Mugge, Robert. *The Return of Rubén Blades* [video-recording]. Mug-Shot Productions, 1988.

Winerip, Michael. "A Rubén Blades Special." *The New York Times Magazine,* vol. 140, June 2, 1991, 46.

INDEX